c.1945, Charles G. Shaw in his New York City studio

I begin with an idea and end with an idea. In between, an involvement of form both loses and finds itself.

CHARLES SHAW

CHARLES G. SHAW

November 1–December 22, 2007

MICHAEL ROSENFELD GALLERY
NEW YORK

UNTITLED (POLYGON CONSTRUCTION), 1939
painted wood relief with artist frame, 17 x 12 x 3 inches, signed

INTRODUCTION
Michael Rosenfeld

Michael Rosenfeld Gallery is honored to present *Charles G. Shaw*, a landmark exhibition featuring major paintings from the first two decades of Shaw's career. Charles Shaw (1892-1971) is highly regarded for the modernist paintings he began to create around 1930, when he shifted the focus of his creative efforts from writing to painting. However, the scope and complexity of Shaw's seminal abstractions from the 1930s and 40s have yet to be explored in depth, and it is my hope that this exhibition will increase awareness and understanding of his career.

Over the past eighteen years, Michael Rosenfeld Gallery has handled numerous Charles Shaw paintings, but this is the gallery's first exhibition devoted to his art. This exhibition came to fruition in January 2006 when the gallery was contacted by Benjamin Carpenter Curcio, grandson of the legendary collector Charles Carpenter (1916-2006), and to whom this exhibition is dedicated. Curcio's interest in Michael Rosenfeld Gallery stemmed from the gallery's reputation for promoting early American abstractionists and for successfully elevating the careers of historic American artists who deserve greater recognition. When I saw the collection, I immediately realized that the gallery had a unique opportunity and I acquired thirty-three paintings that form the core of this show. As I promised Curcio and Charles Carpenter's son, Philip Carpenter, the collection was bought not simply for commercial purposes, but rather to provide a rare and exciting chance to mount a solo exhibition and publish the first significant catalog on his art. I believe that this exhibition and catalog would have delighted Charles Carpenter.

Charles Carpenter was a remarkable man and a visionary collector with impeccable taste and broad interests. Carpenter's collection included Shaker furniture and American silver as well as modern and contemporary art. Among the many artists whose work he acquired were Jean Dubuffet, Ellsworth Kelly, Jackson Pollock, Ad Reinhardt, Andy Warhol, and of course, Charles Shaw. Carpenter was Shaw's close friend, and to his surprise, he became the heir to Shaw's estate, which included paintings from all periods of his career. The paintings featured in *Charles G. Shaw* share the distinguished Charles Carpenter provenance, and they are also remarkable in their exceptional quality. In addition, many of these paintings have not been exhibited since the 1930s and '40s, and several have never been shown at all. Michael Rosenfeld Gallery is honored to exhibit these paintings together for the first time.

I must acknowledge Debra Bricker Balken for her scholarship in the field of American Modernism and the Park Avenue Cubists as well as for her essay for this catalog. I am thankful to Jason Andrew, Associate Director at Michael Rosenfeld Gallery, for his research, which has enabled us to construct an extensive artist chronology. I am also indebted to the many collectors who have acquired Charles Shaw paintings and have generously allowed them to return to the gallery for this exhibition. Finally, I would like to thank the family of Charles Carpenter, particularly Benjamin Carpenter Curcio and Philip Carpenter, for the opportunity to acquire the collection. Their trust in the Michael Rosenfeld Gallery has enabled us to mount this landmark exhibition and to contribute significantly to scholarship on and public awareness of Charles Shaw's life and art.

UNTITLED (INTERSECTING TRAPEZOIDS), c.1936
oil and sand on canvasboard, 18 x 15 inches

CHARLES GREEN SHAW
Debra Bricker Balken

There was detachment in his zeal and
curiosity in his indifference.

—Henry James, *The Ambassadors*

The profundities of poetic influence
need not make poets original; as often
makes them more original, though not
therefore necessarily better.

—Harold Bloom, *The Anxiety of Influence*

When Charles G. Shaw (1892-1974) took up
painting in the late 1920s, his career as a writer—at least, his short, pithy profiles of the denizens of
the New York *beau mode* and literary community—came to an end. Shaw had long since seen writing and painting as separate activities, linked only through the common pursuit, as he put it, of "the
form of the thing."[1] The refinement of a style, or the elaboration of his own singularity and voice,
might have unified his twin occupations, but as Shaw had it, his biographical sketches of figures such
as George Gershwin, F. Scott Fitzgerald, Sinclair Lewis, Anita Loos and Clarence Darrow, were a "different type of communication."[2] Where he would be drawn to the "philosophies and beliefs," as well
as the "subconscious leanings...[and] idiosyncracies"[3] of Darrow, Fitzgerald, and others, rendering
Fitzgerald, for example, as someone who "dances only under pressure, and prefers, at a party to talk
or listen to the chatter of others,"[4] his painting would become far more theoretical and concrete, dis-
possessed of any psychology, while retaining only a sense of the fragmentation that was the primary
inventive feature of these literary sketches.

With the stock market crash of 1929, the market for breezy representations of Jazz-Age authors
and composers had withered, the sartorial features of one's dress, favorite cocktail and club no longer
an apt metaphor for a nation that had been thrown into financial crisis and teetered near social col-
lapse, the unemployment and bread lines now a reality that existed in sharp contrast to his once trans-
formative images or tropes for the quirks and pastimes of the American leisure class. Shaw produced
few such renditions of his friends thereafter, forgoing his associations with *Vanity Fair*, H. L.
Mencken's and Jean George Nathan's *The Smart Set* and *The Bookman* (the latter two publications of
which folded in the early 1930s, casualties of the Depression). Moreover, when Shaw released *Nightlife*
in 1931, a guide to the toniest restaurants, dance halls and hot spots in New York, in addition to being
a veiled or oblique portrait of a City that could still serve a fabulous martini, the book failed to gar-
ner much of an audience, let alone attention, both his mastery of a privileged lifestyle and expertise
as a *bon-vivant* no longer needed. Shaw's own independent means protected him from any personal
economic down-turn but he clearly sensed that his writing had lost its currency, that it failed to touch
on the exigencies of the period. In fact, of the occasional columns that he had written for the *New
Yorker*, a more reflective, less flippant tone registered in his observations of Manhattan in the early
1930s. Writing soon after the publication of *Nightlife* that New York had become a dramatically different place, Shaw remarked that he believed "a tamed and humbler race has evolved; a gentler and
more civil one most certainly."[5] Yet, that did not prevent his stating, in his characteristically terse

schemas of the city, of its architectural permutations and fashions - that he "was happy to learn...that the town has switched from orange to tomato juice."[6]

However, for all of Shaw's gravitation towards the *low-down*, and his reportage of the manners and habits of some of New York's more colorful denizens and their special haunts, he was unforthcoming about the details of his own background and existence. George L. K. Morris, the painter and art critic, who met Shaw in 1935, recalled after his death that he "was the only artist I have encountered who declined ever to talk about himself. I knew Charles for forty years, yet it was always from outside sources that I extracted a little of what his life had been before I first met him."[7] But, there were certain unities that shaped their lives that Morris was too reticent to acknowledge, that he felt should remain unspoken, that might impinge on or detract from the interpretation of Shaw's painting (and by extension, that of his own). Morris might have wanted the *low-down* at the outset of their friendship, that is, the specifics and names of his acquaintances and family, in addition to his addresses, avocations and the cities and countries to which he traveled, but the unstated traits that existed in their upbringing must have made for their instantaneous, deep rapport, accounting, in part, for the long duration of their relationship. Like Morris, Shaw was the scion of a formidable family, an heir to the Woolworth fortune that had been amassed in the late nineteenth century. As Morris, no doubt found out, they were both educated at Yale, although Shaw was thirteen years his senior. And just like Morris, who would become an active contributor to the *Yale Literary Magazine* while an undergraduate, Shaw began his career as a writer by serving on the editorial staff of *The Yale Record*.

While they were both children of privilege, Shaw's early years were far more fraught than Morris's; his mother died when Shaw was three, leaving his care and that of his twin brother to his father and uncle who lived together in an apartment hotel in the Murray Hill section of New York. Shaw remembered that both figures had "retired" before his birth, forgoing their careers in law and commerce, and that his primary education was "formed in the library of our house because they had a very good library and all kinds of books to read...I read a good deal even before going to school."[8] He took to drawing alongside reading, finding in both activities the right match or release for his imagination, solitude also clearly a requisite part of his working practice. Shaw's father would pre-decease his brother by more than two decades and when the latter died in 1928—just as the *The Low-Down* was published – Shaw left New York for Paris and London where he spent two years learning to paint. As he explained towards the end of his life, "I had Paris in my mind or London or both for many, many years. In fact almost from the time I left college. But my uncle was everything to me and I didn't want to leave him alone...the minute things were settled I left."[9]

But this transition in Shaw's life was also beset with professional crisis, the lapsed domestic stability of his life with his uncle—Shaw never married—both liberating and inducing considerable disequilibrium, what with a new found interest in painting competing and impinging on his identity as a writer. How to accommodate both occupations? Moreover, were they compatible and like enterprises? Shaw had studied life drawing at the Arts Students League in the fall of 1926 with Thomas Hart Benton, a figure whose overbearing manner and abundant narcissism must have been alienating to him, as he opted for the less authoritarian and controlling instruction of George Luks with whom he subsequently studied privately. Luks, as Shaw wrote in his profile of the artist that was incorporated into *The Low-Down*, was "a firm upholder in one knowing one's groundwork, he takes little stock in professional dicta."[10] Besides, he was "in no sense a fancy fellow,"[11] as Shaw read him, disdaining the pretensions of his colleagues who maintained and bought into the hegemony of painting, upholding its status as an *über* art. Yet, whatever his overall fondness for Luks, Shaw would soon grasp in Europe the limitations of a methodology that focused on the figure, of an academic training that spurned any pure investigation of form, stating much later, "during those days with George Luks and at the League, I never heard the word abstract mentioned."[12] Although he would never become immersed in the art scene in Paris—that type of engagement would come about later on trips made back to the Continent in the mid-1930s—he picked up on, albeit with some initial hesitation, the modernist ethos that pervaded French culture, noting its deficit not only in his art education but in his own aesthetic outlook. For, in a few of the columns that he wrote for the *New Yorker* after his extensive, sixteen month trip in

Europe, he contrasted the features of New York's built environment with those not only in Paris and London but also in Vienna and Berlin.

Where he once emphatically declared that he "preferred the New York of twenty years ago to the metropolis of the present,"[13] perpetuating the nostalgia and memory of his life before college with his uncle, after he returned to the United States he averred, "I am inclined to agree (reluctantly) with my friend, Paul Morand, that today the best in New York is the most modern. I am still not half as excited by the sight of the Empire State Building as I believe I should be."[14] Morand, a noted French playwright, novelist, poet and diplomat whom he met in Paris, would become one of the influences that contributed to Shaw's tentative conversion to modernism. However, soon after he took up residence again in the Gotham City, this process of relinquishing a once-held romanticism (or a moment in cultural history that no longer existed) would become complete. His painting would now focus on the skyline that he observed from the windows of his apartment in the Drake Hotel on Park Avenue and East 57th Street. Rendered as block-like, towering units of differing scales, these still, spare, unpopulated forms were demarcated by black outlines that were filled with various muted shades of pastel. Like the prose-style of his columns for the *New Yorker*, which drew on his frequent walks from mid-town to the financial district, these austere structures were devoid of any embellishment or detail, succinct statements of the rudiments of architecture. Shaw had briefly studied architecture at Columbia University in 1915, but withdrew after a year, contending that he "was not very happy" with the program, that whatever initial practical motive and desire he might have once (briefly) harbored for some "training"[15] was overwhelmed and dissipated by the technical demands of the profession, with too many compromises and strictures imposed on self-expression.

Shaw would exhibit many of these works at the Valentine Gallery in 1934, his first such public exposure. In the foreword to an accompanying brochure for the show, which was titled *Manhattan Patterns*, Ernest Boyd, a prominent critic and translator who had written a noted monograph on H. L. Mencken in the mid-1920s in addition to numerous articles on aspects of contemporary literature for the *Nation,* yoked these paintings with Shaw's writing, contending, "whether his medium should be paint and canvas or prose, I suspect that his retort in this case would be that of George Moore [the Irish novelist], who said: 'It does not matter how badly you paint, so long as you don't paint badly like other people.'"[16] However, Henry McBride—a veteran advocate of American modernism, who had consistently reviewed the work of artists associated with the circle of Alfred Stieglitz as well as the New York Dadaists from the early 1920s onwards—found no hint of derivation or incompetence in Shaw's flat, semi-abstract architectonic shapes, countering Boyd's rhetorical comparisons and off-handed ambivalence. In his column for the *New York Sun*, he found that Shaw's "treatment throughout is bold and nonimitative, the lines and planes created solely to fit a self-imposed design. Nor is there any suggestion of either the literary or the sentimental, the personnel [sic] reigning supreme."[17]

Manhattan Patterns might have generated widespread press, as it was featured in most of the city's daily newspapers, but it certainly evaded A. E. Gallatin, the founder of the Gallery of Living Art in 1927. Gallatin's project, which was located at New York University on Washington Square East, represented the first showcase for contemporary art in New York, predating the formation of the Museum of Modern Art by over two years. Through its permanent installations of work by Picasso, Braque, Gris, Léger and later, Mondrian, Arp and others, the Gallery provided for many artists who lived in proximity to the site their first introduction to the pivotal developments in European modernism, that is, to the radical pictorial inventions that either dissolved or dispensed with the figure as an aesthetic starting point. Gallatin, with characteristic hauteur, and a certain condescension, acquiesced to visit Shaw's studio in early 1935, after the prodding of a fellow Union Club member. As an acknowledged arbiter of taste, or as George L. K. Morris had said of him, "what he had was an eye," that elusive knack to identify the hallmarks of "quality,"[18] (a long since spurned term given its aloofness and accrued resistance to codification or any specific meaning), Gallatin, of course, was disinclined towards his friend's recommendation, passing off his superficial acquaintance of art as a tell-tale limitation. But when he arrived at the Drake Hotel, at which Shaw's apartment doubled as both living quarters and as a studio, he ineffably knew that he had encountered an artist who was "doing the most important work in abstract painting in America today."[19] (Morris had also noted that Gallatin was handicapped by an inability to be "expressive,"[20] that his terse verbal pronouncements inhibited any sustained critical analysis or descriptive elaboration. Or, as Morris observed, "He never could tell you why he liked anything or why anything was good or why something else was bad. He'd just say it was bad...and that was the best he could do."[21])

Gallatin's visit followed with a repeat meeting a few days thereafter, to which he invited Morris to join him. Morris, a young artist who had been made the curator of the Gallery of Living Art in 1931, responded with similar alacrity to Shaw's compact reductions of New York's architecture, recognizing their unmatched pictorial intelligence, their serene yet rigorous recasting of basic shapes into novel compositions that stretched and reworked the precepts of Cubism. Shaw, of course, had encountered the work of Picasso, Braque and other modernist figures on his trip to Paris in 1929, their daring restatements of form becoming an integral part of his new aesthetic epiphany or revelation. Yet Morris was equally surprised to learn that he "had no connection with New York artists who worked in his direction,"[22] that his contacts remained essentially literary, a circumstance that heightened the originality of his painting, its isolation from a critical dialogue a primary feature of its novelty. Moreover, his manner of dress, and overall deportment, set him off from Morris's received notions of an artist, confounding stereotypes that related to a counter-cultural image, an impression that was all the more striking given that Morris himself hardly deviated from conformity when it came to etiquette, and clothes. As he remembered Shaw soon after his death in 1974, "he was well over six feet tall and sturdily built. His appearance was always elegant, with a neatly trimmed mustache and a slightly florid countenance. He might have passed as one of the elusive characters in a British spy movie...he was different from other artists I have known."[23]

Shaw himself noted that his life before he met Gallatin and Morris was bereft of artistic connections, notwithstanding his association with George Luks (who died in 1933 on the eve of Shaw's exhibition at Valentine Gallery), and that of all his literary friends, moreover, "I don't think there was a single one that really cared a hoot about contemporary painting. Not one."[24] Shaw maintained contact with Mencken, Nathan, Loos, Boyd and figures such as George Gershwin and Cole Porter, a classmate from Yale, who would refer to him as "Immense Man" or "Big Boy" in their correspondence,[25] thus underscoring that Morris's conception of his stature was staggering and universally shared. But his dual pursuits of painting and writing would always remain socially separate, compartmentalized worlds, with the salient exception of his new relationships with Morris and Gallatin, for whom these vocations were more entwined, part of the business of becoming a complete and well-versed intellectual. Morris, for instance, had co-founded *The Miscellany* with Dwight McDonald, Geoffrey Hellman and Frederick Dupee (all classmates from Yale) in the early 1930s. Their bi-monthly literary journal would presage the cultural section of the *Partisan Review*, of which Morris also became an editor when it was re-structured in late 1937, writing its columns on art alongside Clement Greenberg through 1942. (The leftist, initially pro-Trotskyite political orientation of *Partisan Review* was lost on Morris, who contended, "it was radically politically, and I produced the radical art."[26]) Similarly, Gallatin, for all of his ascribed verbal shortcomings, produced an ongoing spate of publications from 1910s onwards—short studies that would track his evolving modernist interests, eventually incorporating figures such as Charles Demuth and John Marin into his purview in advance of the four successive publications he brought out to document the growing collections of the Gallery of Living Art.

But, unlike his new friends, Shaw remained disaffected of writing art criticism, or even a short monograph on another artist. While he maintained that painting was certainly capable of being spun into theory, as well as being parsed, described and situated in a historic continuum—Shaw, after all, was a formalist who abided by a belief in a progressive art history, of a linear or teleological unfolding and succession of styles – he resisted projecting his own ego on the vast and divergent subjects and forms of art, claiming that "I agree with Goethe who said artists don't talk they paint...I have known so many people who could talk beautifully but they never did much about painting. They worked it all off in words."[27] In fact, it was this attribute that deeply attracted him to Gallatin, believing, like Morris, that, "he had the finest eye...of any person I have ever known. Of being able to tell a first rate painting, an abstract painting in particular. He said once to me he didn't know how he did it."[28] This emphasis on Gallatin's intuition, on the connoisseur's insight and ability to instantaneously grasp and identify the intangible presence of "quality" in a work of art, was a characteristic, or honed talent, which Shaw would continue to insist throughout his career could not be commodified or pinned down, which had no material component or form, however unambiguous, spartan, controlled and clear his own paintings from 1933 onward, their compositional ingredients conjuring many obvious equivalents that could be put into prose. Moreover, his own painting, like that of Morris's and later Gallatin's – the latter of whom who did not take up art until 1936—had no metaphysical content or interest in transcendence where the avoidance of words might be understandable, his craft ironically an agency for the distillation and arrangement of concrete, specific (largely) geometric shapes.

However, there were other telling aspects to Gallatin and his remarkable "eye" to which Shaw also responded, further forging and deepening their connections. For example, Shaw engaged in a certain self-description when he declared after Gallatin's death that "Albert Eugene remained in many ways a being of the nineteenth century. Indeed, save for his interest in the plastic arts, it was the nineteenth, rather than the twentieth century, at least ideationally, he preferred."[29] Shaw's own penchant for a decade that ended with the rise of the first World War, for the waning years of the age of innocence, echo and run through this reminiscence, while reinforcing a mutual longing for an earlier stage in life that seemed immutable—features that became transposed in their painting through a quest for formal purity, rendering, as Shaw had, the New York skyline as inert, symmetrical, and stabile.

Gallatin was so taken by Shaw and his work that he amended his mandate at the Gallery of Living Art to include temporary exhibitions, disturbing the once quasi-permanence of the installations of his ever-expanding collection and its historic sketch of the trajectories of modernist art. In late spring of 1935, Shaw inaugurated this series, with Gallatin writing in the accompanying press release, "It is most refreshing to find a native American developing both an abstract feeling and technique in an original manner."[30] Shortly thereafter, the two traveled to Europe, one of the first such trips that Shaw made with a friend, generally preferring to be on his own, his privacy always paramount, a detail that succeeded in shrouding many of the circumstances and arc of his biography in secrecy.[31] He found Gallatin to be "a very companionable fellow," although, he qualified the uniqueness of their camaraderie, noting that "other people had a hard time of it...we clicked alright."[32] The trip was expansive, incorporating visits to Swiss, Italian, German and Scandinavian museums in addition to sites in London and Paris. It was in Paris that Shaw finally visited the studios of Picasso, Léger, Braque, Jean Hélion and Jean Arp, among others, with the latter two artists eventually becoming his friends. Moreover, Arp and Hélion would exert noticeable influence on his aesthetic thinking, adding to his evolving understanding of the nomenclature and terms used to define the various off-shoots and permutations of Cubist painting, adumbrating manifold subtleties and differences. For instance, in 1936, Shaw worked simultaneously on a series of shaped canvases, or "plastic polygons," as he called them, as well as compositions that drew on interlocking biomorphic forms, references to the alternatively planar, rectilinear and organic elements that populated the paintings of *Art Concret* and *Abstraction-Creation* groups of which Hélion and Arp were leading members. The word "plastic," no doubt, was one that he inherited from both artists, an amalgam of appropriations, alluding to the wood relief constructions that Arp produced from the late-1920s onwards (and which Shaw would later consciously mimic), as well as the title of a journal, *Plastique*, that Morris and Gallatin co-founded and edited with the Swiss artist in 1937, and which had initially been suggested and named by Hélion. Shaw's "plastic polygons" represented the first shaped canvases produced in the United States, predating the work of numerous Minimalists painters in the late 1950s and early 1960s, becoming truly radical pictorial statements, the likes of which were unknown in the United States. He explained the transformation of his earlier abstractions of New York's soaring architectural structures, which still retained a sense of space, however compressed and limited, as a logical outcome, ceding to "the rigid tranquility of a sidewalk pattern viewed from above. Distance has yielded to design; depth has surrendered to a wall of equal planes. For what it acquired in purity, it had wholly lost in three-dimensional value."[33] Moreover, he contended that these elegant reductions of vertical bands of color were wholly American in invention, "sprouting, so to speak, from the steel and concrete of New York City... That in its growth and development it no longer embraces those somewhat realistic features found in its progenitor is of no moment. Structurally and functionally it is solely of America."[34]

Yet Shaw would also elide or morph his designation "plastic" into another equally descriptive term, "concrete," which was similarly used in the *very few* statements that he wrote on his work to offset and distinguish its meanings from that of the sometimes misused, yet opposite connotations of "abstract" art. In fact, in 1936, a pivotal year for Shaw and his increasing public advocacy for the cause and singularly of the American reverberations of modernist painting, he proposed the term "concretionist" to Gallatin for the title of an off-site exhibition that he was in the throes of staging at the Paul Reinhardt Galleries to protest the conceptual thrust of Alfred Barr's landmark project, *Cubism and Abstract Art*, at the Museum of Modern Art that spring. Shaw had some inside intelligence or advance warning that Barr's sweeping overview of modernism would exclude most Americans, its Eurocentric orientation conveyed in a telephone conversation Shaw had with Barr in his new capacity as a member of the Museum's Advisory Committee (a role that he shared with Morris). Not only was he "very disappointed"[35] by Barr's construction of modernism and of its implicit diminishment of American developments, but he actively worked with Gallatin to assemble his rejoinder, contributing his advice on a roster of artists. The exhibition, which became titled *Five Contemporary American Concretionists*, was composed of work by Charles Biederman, Alexander Calder, John Ferren, Morris and Shaw, with Calder as the only figure who made his way into Barr's reformulation of the School of Paris, its stylistic genealogies and contemporary expansions now even more complex. Shaw, no doubt, knew of Hélion's applications of the word "concrete," as did Gallatin, who had hired the French artist as a part-time consultant, and of its embodiment of formal specificity when it came to painting. It provided the right theoretical hook or contrast, moreover, to Barr's more rambling, diffuse prescriptions, further distinguishing the artists in Gallatin's show. As Shaw elaborated in an interview, "the word 'abstract,' even today to some people who ought to know better, use it entirely wrong, [when] applied to the field of painting. They think of it as an abstract idea. The word should have been extract and that is why I wanted to make it more to the point and call it concrete."[36]

Shaw and Morris would eventually resign from the Advisory Board of the Museum of Modern Art in 1941, no longer able to countenance Barr's predisposition towards Europe and his ongoing American exclusions. Henry McBride, who continued to remain interested in Shaw's work, wrote in the *New York Sun* that the artists who made up Gallatin's project should be "world-ranking," opening with a headline, "America Also Goes Abstract."[37] The finer distinctions between the "concrete" and "abstract" might have been lost on McBride although his contention clearly rested with Barr and his omissions. However, Edward Alden Jewell of the *The New York Times* would write what would become a more entrenched impression, passing the show off as an "Academism of the Left,"[38] while maintaining a consistent institutional bias that would be perpetuated by numerous subsequent critics. Whatever the bold individuality of Shaw's *plastic polygon* series, his work thereafter would be frequently construed as derivative, a pale iteration of French formal ingenuity, oblivious to its refinements and the nuances of its discourses. In 1936, Shaw, again along with Morris, would also become a founding member of the American Abstract Artists (AAA) group, an artist's run organization that banded together to seek exhibition opportunities in the wake of Barr's perceived aesthetic tyranny. However, the negative reception to their work had also become compounded by the rise of new movements and artists. While Shaw might have later declared that, "I avoided politics as the plague all of my life,"[39] he did, in fact, become embroiled in one of the most urgent and hard-won artistic debates in American cultural history. He wrote to his detractors with uncharacteristic emotion in the 1938 *Yearbook* of the AAA, knowing their critical allegiances had shifted to so-called Regionalist painting and to Thomas Hart Benton, the teacher he snubbed at the Art Students League, that "art, since its inception, has never, depended upon realism. Why, one cannot help wondering, should it begin now?"[40] But George L. K. Morris was better able than Shaw, and for that matter, Gallatin, to enunciate and focus the real terms of this crisis, stating in the same *Yearbook* that "the derogatory charges of European imitation that you will have to face present a purely modern and journalistic brand of criticism. In no other period was the artist expected to appear, full-armed, as by spontaneous combustion. Can it be that Raphael was derided for imitating Perugino? Durer, Rubens, or Poussin for incorporating the art of Italy into their own?" [41]

Shaw would continue to exhibit actively in the late 1930s and beyond, both with the AAA through their annual exhibitions, as well as with Gallatin, Morris and Suzy Frelinghuysen (Morris's wife who took up painting soon after their marriage in 1935) becoming a quartet known as the "Park Avenue Cubists," their economic circumstances always a barrier for their far less advantaged friends. And, although Shaw would also be awarded two exhibitions at the Solomon R. Guggenheim Museum in the early 1940s, they would go unnoticed, with critics such as Harold Rosenberg later maintaining that "formally, the thirties were a drop-out; though there appeared an immense effusion of craft skill: not one new aesthetic idea emerged." [42] This type of setback awaited its corrections. The charges of imitation would later be construed in the early 1980s as wrong-headed and off, a vital part of the reinvigoration of modernism and its subsequent post-historic counterparts.

Debra Bricker Balken is an independent curator and writer who works on subjects relating to American modernism and contemporary art. Her projects have been presented at the Whitney Museum of American Art, Los Angeles County Museum of Art, Des Moines Art Center, and the Phillips Collection, in addition to university museums such as MIT List Visual Arts Center, the Grey Art Gallery, the Wexner Center for the Arts, and the Institute of Contemporary Art/Philadelphia. She is currently completing a book on the American Art Critic, Harold Rosenberg, for the University of Chicago Press. The author would like to acknowledge the research assistance of Jason Andrew.

ENDNOTES

1. Paul Cummings, *Interview with Charles Shaw,* April 15, 1968. Archives of American Art, Smithsonian Institution, 21.
2. *Ibid.*
3. Charles G. Shaw, "Foreword," *The Low-Down* (New York: Henry Holt and Company, 1928), v, vi.
4. Shaw, "F. Scott Fitzgerald," *Ibid.,* 166.
5. Charles G. Shaw, "Return to New York, After a Sixteen Months' Absence," *The New Yorker,* February 14, 1931, 18.
6. *Ibid.*
7. George L. K. Morris, "Charles Green Shaw," *The Century Yearbook: 1975* (New York: The Century Association, 1975), 281. Morris was clearly unfamiliar with Shaw's early history, claiming that he lived abroad during the decade of the 1920s, 282.
8. Shaw, quoted in Cummings, 1.
9. *Ibid.,* 10.
10. Shaw, "George Luks," *The Low-Down,* 92.
11. *Ibid.,* 90.
12. Shaw, quoted in Cummings, 9.
13. Charles G. Shaw, "How I Feel About Things," *The New Yorker,* June 1, 1929, 26.
14. Shaw, "Return to New York."
15. Shaw, quoted in Cummings, 10.
16. Ernest Boyd, "Foreword," *Manhattan Patterns by Charles G. Shaw,* exh. brochure (New York: Valentine Gallery, 1934), n.p.
17. Henry McBride, "Charles G. Shaw," *The New York Sun,* March 31, 1934.
18. Paul Cummings, *Interview with George L. K. Morris,* December 11, 1968. Archives of American Art, Smithsonian Institution, 8.
19. "Charles G. Shaw Has One Man Exhibition at New York University's Gallery of Living Art," New York University press release, April 27, 1935. Charles G. Shaw Papers, Archives of American Art, Smithsonian Institution. On the circumstances that surrounded Shaw's meeting Gallatin, cf. Debra Bricker Balken, "The Park Avenue Cubists: Gallatin, Morris, Frelinghuysen and Shaw," in *The Park Avenue Cubists,* exh. catalogue (New York: Grey Art Gallery, and London; Ashgate, 2002), 3ff.
20. Morris, quoted in Cummings, 8.
21. *Ibid.*
22. Morris, "Charles Green Shaw," 284.
23. *Ibid.,* 283.
24. Morris, quoted in Cummings, 31.
25. Cole Porter, quoted in Buck Pennington, "The "Floating World," in the Twenties: The Jazz Age and Charles Green Shaw," *Archives of American Art Journal,* vol. 20, no. 4 (1980), 21.
26. Morris, quoted in Cummings, 12.
27. Shaw, quoted in Cummings, 26.
28. *Ibid.,* 11.
29. Charles G. Shaw, "Albert Eugene Gallatin: A Reminiscence," *The Princeton University Library Chronicle,* vol. XIV, no. 3 (Spring 1953), 135.
30. "Charles G. Shaw Has One Man Exhibition at New York University's Gallery of Living Art."
31. Shaw's journals were donated along with his papers to the Archives of American Art, making his daily activities from 1919 to 1972 known and available to the public. However, as Pennington, observed, they contain little "embellishment," 22, that is, little emotional or psychological content.
32. Shaw, quoted in Cummings, 15.
33. Charles G. Shaw, "The Plastic Polygon," *Plastique,* no. 3 (Spring 1938), 28.
34. *Ibid.* 29.
35. Charles Green Shaw diary, vol. 1X, February 3, 1936, 225. Shaw Papers. Cited in Gail Stavitsky, "A Landmark Exhibition: Five Contemporary American Concretionists, March 1936," *Archives of American Art Journal,* vol. 33, no.2 (1993), 3.
36. Shaw, quoted in Cummings, 25.
37. Henry McBride, "America Also Goes Abstract," *New York Sun,* March 14, 1936.
38. Edward Alden Jewell, "The Realm of Art: Academism of the Left," *The New York Times,* March 15, 1936, 8x.
39. *Ibid.,* 15.
40. Charles G. Shaw, "A Word to the Objector," *1938 AAA Yearbook* (New York: Privately Published), n.p.
41. George L. K. Morris, "Some Personal Letters to American Artists Recently Exhibiting in New York," *Partisan Review,* vol. IX, no. 4 (March 1938), 25.
42. Harold Rosenberg, "The Thirties," reprinted in *The De-Definition of Art* (Chicago: University of Chicago Press, 1972), 180.

CHARLES G. SHAW

A SELECTION OF PAINTINGS
FROM THE 1930s AND 1940s

UNTITLED (CUBIST STILL-LIFE WITH GLASS), c.1932
oil and sand on canvasboard, 16 x 12 inches, signed

UNTITLED (CUBIST COMPOSITION WITH GUITAR), c.1932
oil on canvas, 20 x 16 ¼ inches, signed

UNTITLED (CUBIST COMPOSITION WITH TELEPHONE), c.1932
oil on canvas, 24 x 20 inches, signed

UNTITLED (CUBIST TEAPOT), c.1934
oil and sand on canvas, 18 x 15 inches, signed

UNTITLED (CONDUCTOR), c.1934
oil on canvas, 30 x 22 inches, signed

UNTITLED (FOURTH OF JULY), c.1934
oil on canvas, 30 x 22 inches, signed

LITERARY BLASPHEMES: PORTRAIT OF ERNEST BOYD, 1934
oil on canvas, 28 x 24 inches

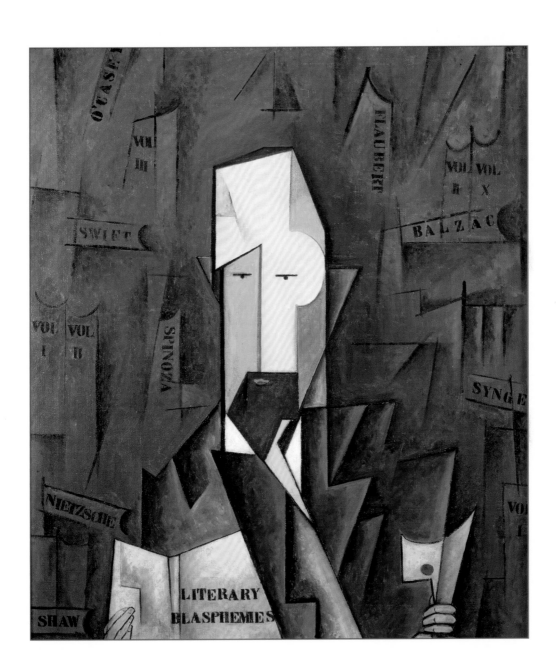

UNTITLED, 1935
oil and sand on canvas, 28 x 24 inches, signed

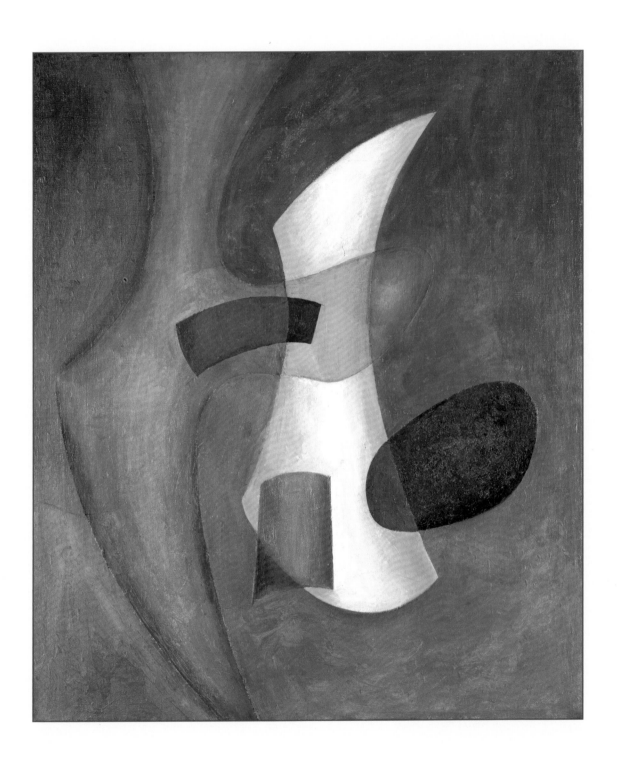

UNTITLED (ORGANIC CUBIST ABSTRACTION), c.1935
oil on canvas, 28 x 24 inches, signed

UNTITLED (ORGANIC CUBIST ABSTRACTION), c.1935
oil on canvas, 36 x 30 inches, signed

UNTITLED (PLASTIC POLYGON ABSTRACT FORM), 1935
oil on canvas, 28 x 24 inches, signed

UNTITLED (PLASTIC POLYGON ABSTRACT FORM), 1935
oil on canvas, 28 x 24 inches, signed

PLASTIC POLYGON ABSTRACT FORM "NO. 6", 1936
oil on canvas, 15 1/8 x 18 inches, signed

UNTITLED (INTERSECTING TRAPEZOIDS NO.2), c.1936
oil on canvasboard, 18 x 15 inches

UNTITLED (INTERSECTING TRAPEZOIDS NO.1), c.1936
oil and sand on canvasboard, 18 x 15 inches

UNTITLED (ABSTRACT MASK), 1935
oil on canvas, 17 1/8 x 15 7/8 inches, signed

POLYGON "NO. 34", 1937
painted wood relief with artist frame, 22 ¼ x 28 ¼ x 1 ¾ inches, signed

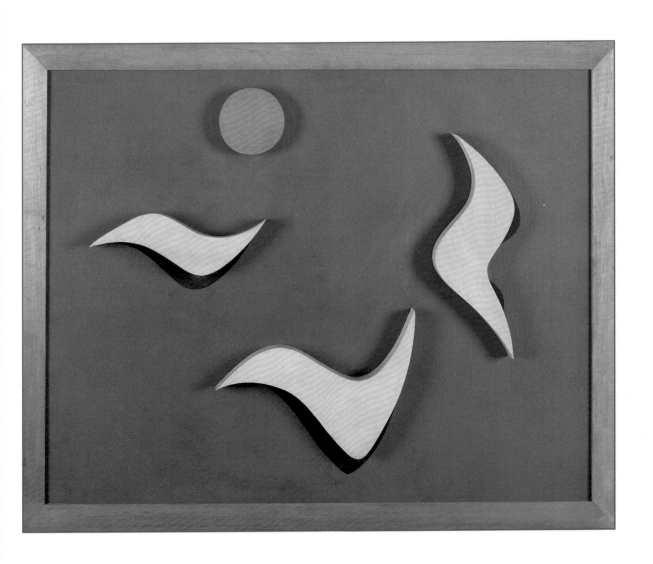

UNTITLED (RED AND BLUE ABSTRACTION), c.1937
oil on canvas, 20 x 24 inches, signed

UNTITLED (POLYGON), c.1937
oil and sand on canvas, 17 x 20 inches

UNTITLED, 1937
oil and sand on panel with artist frame, 32 ¼ x 20 ¾ x 1 ½ inches

UNTITLED, c.1940
oil on wood, 11 x 16 ½ x 1 ¼ inches

UNTITLED, 1940
oil on canvasboard, 16 x 11 7/8 inches, signed

UNTITLED I, 1940
oil on canvasboard, 16 x 12 inches, signed

NON - OBJECTIVE ORGANIZATION - I, 1940
oil on canvasboard, 18 x 14 ¾ inches, signed

UNTITLED, c.1940
oil on canvasboard, 20 x 16 inches, signed

UNTITLED, 1940
oil on canvasboard, 16 x 12 inches, signed

54)

UNTITLED, 1941
oil on canvasboard, 16 x 12 inches, signed

UNTITLED (GEOMETRIC ABSTRACTION), 1942
oil on Masonite, 22 x 30 inches, signed

UNTITLED (ATOMIC FLIGHT), 1945
oil on canvasboard, 22 x 30 inches, signed

ATOMIC FLIGHT, 1946
oil on canvasboard, 22 x 30 inches, signed

NANTUCKET WHARF - NO.2, 1947
oil on canvasboard, 30 x 22 inches, signed

NANTUCKET WATERFRONT - NO.3, 1948
oil and sand on Masonite, 50 x 32 inches, signed

CHARLES G. SHAW

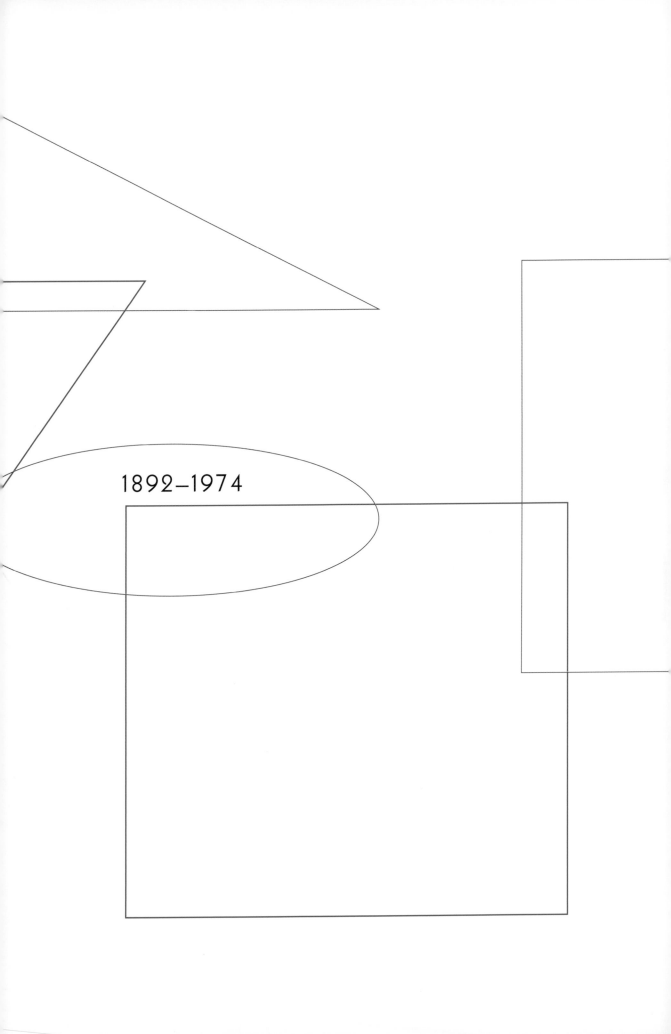

1892–1974

1892

On May 1, Charles Green Shaw, Jr. is born in New York City. He is named after his father, a descendant of early Quakers who immigrated to the United States from England in 1697, settling first in Northampton, Bucks County, PA and moving to New York City in the mid-nineteenth century. Shaw's father was from Madison, IN, and his mother Eva Kennedy Morris was born in Louisville, KY. His parents died when he was young and upon their deaths, Shaw received an inheritance based partly on the fortune of the F.W. Woolworth Company, one of the twentieth century's largest retail chains worldwide. Shaw and his twin brother Frank were raised by their uncle, Frank D. Shaw, in New York City.

1901

By age nine, Shaw is already an avid artist. He assembles one hundred colored illustrations for his first book, *The Costumes of Nations*. He is also an avid collector of stamps and attends the theater often. Shaw attends Friends Seminary (1903-1904, 4th Class and 1904-1905, 5th Class), a private Quaker school located in downtown Manhattan, and later the Berkeley School. While at school, he is active in sports, including baseball, basketball, hockey, and tennis. Shaw is the captain of the football team. Letters and correspondence reveal that Shaw moved freely in the high society during his youth.

1906-1908

Cubism begins in Paris.

1910-1914

In the years before World War I, Shaw works briefly in the real estate business and becomes prominently known as a member of café society[1] and a "man about town." "His cards of invitation and his journal suggest that he had access to all the 'right' people and social events. He regularly passed Christmas night dancing at Mrs. W.K. Vanderbilt's Christmas ball; summers were spent playing tennis at Newport or swimming off Block Island."[2]

1914

The Whitney Studio is established by Gertrude Vanderbilt Whitney at 147 West Fourth Street. The facility was established as a place where young artists could exhibit their work. An early activist for young American art, Gertrude Vanderbilt Whitney was an artist herself. From the Whitney Studio, her legacy would develop into the Whitney Studio Club (1918-28) to the Whitney Galleries (1928-30), and the Whitney Museum of American Art (1931).

World War I begins, and Shaw graduates with a B.A. in Philosophy from the Sheffield Scientific School at Yale College in New Haven, CT. While at Yale, he contributes to numerous publications and is a member of the editorial staff and art contributor at *The Yale Record*, America's oldest college humor magazine (founded in 1872). "During his college career he contributed many commendable writings to various publications and upon the completion of his schooling, entered the advertising business as an editorial writer."[3]

1915

Shaw enrolls in Columbia University's School of Architecture but withdraws after only one year.

1916

In the spring, Shaw's first piece of published writing appears in *Smart Set*, a highly regarded literary magazine founded by writer H.L. Mencken and drama critic George Jean Nathan, both friends of Shaw. The publication was credited for introducing readers to American modernism through the writings of F. Scott Fitzgerald, Eugene O'Neil, Sinclair Lewis, Carl Van Vechten and Maxwell Anderson. Shaw's contribution was a fictional depiction of the horrors of a camping trip. From July 12 to August 8, Shaw completes a

1915, Shaw summering in Lenox, Massachusetts

1918, Lieutenant Charles G. Shaw of the 335th Aerial Squad

training session at the Military Instruction Camp held under the auspices of the War Department of the United States in Plattsburgh, NY. While at training camp, Shaw grows a moustache, a feature that would identify him for the rest of his life.

1917

The U.S. enters World War I. Shaw becomes the assistant editor of *The Chronicle*. He enlists on September 27 and attends the Aviation Officers Training School in San Antonio, Texas. On his enlistment papers, his vocation is noted as Editor.

1918

In January, Shaw is commissioned in the Army Air Force, and in August, after several months at the flying fields in Garden City (NY) and Morrison (VA), he sails to England, where he serves for six months as a Lieutenant with the 335th Aero Squadron in Stockbridge, Hampshire. In December, a month after the armistice with Germany was signed, Shaw returns to the U.S. He receives an honorable discharge on January 3, 1919. Upon his return to civilian life, Shaw accepts a position with the real estate firm of Ladd & Nichols in New York City. He becomes a member of the St. Nicholas Club, St. Anthony Club, Columbia University Club and Delta Psi Fraternity.

1919

The Treaty of Versailles is signed on June 28.
Shaw writes the lyrics of a musical comedy for which Deems Taylor,[4] an acclaimed composer and critic, contributes the score.

In the years before World War I, Shaw works briefly in the real estate business and becomes prominently known as a member of café society[1] and a "man about town."

67

1923

A romantic liaison with leading show girl and actress Jane Carroll ensues. Shaw writes to her frequently from various locales including a café in France.

1926

In October, Shaw studies with Thomas Hart Benton in an afternoon class at the Art Students League of New York. He later studies privately at the studio of George Luks, who becomes a close friend. Until this time, Shaw's art consisted mostly of caricatures and line drawings, often executed to illustrate his articles. Deep-sea fishing is a favorite pastime, and by the late twenties, Shaw had fished the waters off Maine, Long Island, New York, Florida, and Cuba.

At this time, Shaw resides at 417 Park Avenue in New York City.

1927

On December 12, Albert E. Gallatin opens The Gallery of Living Art. Occupying three specially-constructed alcoves in the South Study Hall at New York University, The Gallery of Living Art becomes the first permanent public collection of abstract art in the U.S. providing "an informal atmosphere for intellectual exchange, as well as a place where artists could congregate and study the newest developments in European art."[5]

Shaw's first novel, *Heart in a Hurricane* (New York: Brentano's), is published. The novel chronicles the adventures of I. Robert Twombley who, after post-graduate work at Crio's, the Savoy, and the cafes of the Riviera, returns to New Port and New York for his final degree of Doctor of Leisure. F. Scott Fitzgerald, loved the book, writing to Shaw on June 21, 1927: "It is a damn good piece of humorous writing from end to end much better than anything of its sort I've read in years."[6] At this time, Shaw has found much success as a writer, reporting on the social scene for magazines that include *The New Yorker, Vanity Fair, Smart Set, Harper's Bazaar,* and *Town & Country.* His writing, as well as his social pedigree, enabled contact with such notables as Clarence Darrow, F. Scott Fitzgerald, George Gershwin, Sinclair Lewis, Anita Loos, Dorothy Parker, and Monty Wooley.

1928

The death of Shaw's uncle has an emotional impact on him. Shaw's play *What Next!* opens

c.1925, Shaw in Havana, Cuba with Cole Porter and an unidentified friend

in New York City with a very brief run. He also publishes his second book *The Low Down* (New York: Henry Holt & Co.), a collection of articles based on interviews with New York literary figures and show-business celebrities including Michael Strange, Sinclair Lewis, George Jean Nathan, and Adele Astaire. He summers in Newport (RI).

1929

The Museum of Modern Art is founded. Alfred H. Barr, Jr. is its first director. On October 24, the New York Stock market crashes. Shaw is unaffected. His journal entry for this date mentions only that he "read in the papers of the worst Wall Street Panic in 20 years." His ideas to protect his own financial security are: "1. Return to handmade articles. 2. Limit purchasing on credit. 3. Cut down on women employment."[7]

Shaw develops the "plastic polygon form." The plastic polygons are to be his most influential and well-known series.

1929-1930

In August, Shaw leaves New York on an extended trip to Europe. He spends only one month in Paris. From Paris, Shaw moves on to London in late September, living at 4 Eungmore Street, Rutland Gate. Shaw would later declare, "My painting career began during my residence in Paris [1929]."

In December 1930, Shaw returns to New York as a painter.[8] However, he continues to write, publishing *Nightlife: Vanity Fair's Guide to New York After Dark* (New York: John Day Company) in the fall of 1931. Given the extent of postwar economic devastation, *Nightlife* "must have seemed very shallow in the context of the nation's struggle for economic survival."[9]

1931

Gertrude Vanderbilt Whitney establishes The Whitney Museum of American Art. While the collection favors the art of the revolutionary artists derisively called the Ashcan School (among them John Sloan, George Luks, and Everett Shinn), as well as realists (Edward Hopper) and scene painters (John Steuart Curry and Thomas Hart Benton), Ms. Whitney's initial gift is comprised of many important works by early American modernists including Stuart Davis, Charles Demuth, Charles Sheeler, Max Weber, and others.

1932

Shaw returns to Paris, where he visits museums and galleries. During the first week, he surveyed thirteen galleries and was particularly impressed by the work of Cézanne and Picasso.[10] At this time, Shaw's own artistic style evolves from an overt imitation of Cubism to a style inspired by Synthetic Cubism through simplified, geometric images. The economic state of the country, now in the depths of the Great Depression, "provides little outlet for further articles on glitzy nightclubs and restaurants."[11]

Shaw's fourth book, *Lady by Chance* (New York: McCaulay), is published.

1933

Shaw develops the "plastic polygon form," which he describes in an essay of the same name as a "several sided figure divided into a broken pattern of rectangles."[12] The plastic polygons are to be his most influential and well-known series.

1934

On April 2, Shaw's first solo exhibition of paintings, *Manhattan Patterns by Charles G. Shaw,* opens at Valentine Gallery in New York City. The exhibition is announced and reviewed in nearly every contemporary daily or weekly, including *The New Yorker, American Art News, Art Digest, The Daily Mirror, The Wall Street Journal, New York Evening Post* and *The New York Times.*

The *New York Herald Tribune* writes, "The popular Charlie Shaw is having the first exhibition of his paintings this week at the Valentine Gallery [...] He has called his exhibition "Manhattan Patterns" [...] for the two dozen or more paintings were all inspired by different aspects of our kaleidoscopic city. Charlie Shaw is tall, dark, handsome...at one

Mannequin, c.1934

time he wrote a column on a leading New York newspaper, and he has written several books and dozens of amusing magazine articles. Charlie is a gourmet [...] knows a great deal about food and wines and has managed to have a placid and extremely pleasant life. He's lived in England a good deal and has acquired a very British and philosophical attitude. Incidentally, he's an inveterate 'first nighter' and is often accompanied by George Jean Nathan, the well-known critic."

The critic Ernest Boyd writes a foreword for the exhibition brochure: "Charles G. Shaw's Manhattan Patterns are once more an illustration of the fascination of the New York scene, the New York skyscape, for the eye and imagination of the artist [...] It is bold, nonimitative and intensely personal [...] he sees the detail, but paints in large, ample and vigorous strokes in which all details are comprehended and synthesizes. That is as it should be, for such is the way in which Manhattan endears herself. In a pink haze of summer loveliness, or in the murky coziness of a winter evening, she asks one to forget her defective details and respond to her total charm."[13]

The New York Sun extols: "The canvases of Charles G. Shaw depict the New York scene in a hitherto unexpressed manner. They are, for the most part, semi-abstract in character and emphasize simplicity plus a novel employment of planes. By a free adoption of the Gotham background, Mr. Shaw has sought to accent new forms." (March 31)

1935

George L. K. Morris writes, "He might have passed as one of the elusive characters in a British spy movie; at any rate, he was a different type from other artists I have known."

In April, Shaw meets Albert E. Gallatin through a mutual friend.[14] Upon seeing Shaw's work Gallatin declares, "Mr. Shaw is doing the most important work in abstract painting in American today." Gallatin breaks his rule against mounting one-person exhibitions at The Gallery of Living Art. George L.K. Morris assists in the selection of the works for Shaw's one-man show, which runs from May 1 to October 1. The press release explains: "The Gallery's rule against one man shows was broken...because of the important place Mr. Shaw now occupies among American abstract painters."[15]

The *New York Evening Post* reports, "The Gallery of Living Art at New York University has broken a long standing rule and is devoting part of its wall space to a special one-man exhibition of paintings by Charles G. Shaw, American abstractionist" (April 27).

According to Morris, "Charlie changed very little from then (1935) until his final years. He was well over six feet tall and sturdily built. His appearance was elegant, with a neatly trimmed mustache and a slightly florid countenance. He might have passed as one of the elusive characters in a British spy movie; at any rate, he was a different type from other artists I have known. He had perfect manners and obviously new his way around the world; and he had what Gertrude Stein called 'the gift of intimacy.'"[16]

Self Portrait, 1935

Now an integral member of the budding American abstractionists, that summer Shaw travels to Paris with Gallatin and Morris, where he visits the studios of Picasso, Braque, and Léger and meets, among others, Jean Arp, John Ferren, and Jean Hélion. "The largely self-taught Shaw [...] received accolades from Arp whose work exerted a considerable influence upon him."[17]

In November, Shaw accompanies Gallatin, who is making selections for a show of American abstractionists, to the studio of Charles Biederman.[18]

At this time, Shaw resides at the Drake Hotel, 440 Park Avenue in New York City.

1936

Gallatin renames his Gallery of Living Art to Museum of Living Art.

Shaw becomes a founding member of the American Abstract Artists group (AAA), exhibiting his art and rallying support for American abstraction which at the time had been consistently met with distain from art critics and the public.[19] Shaw accepts a position on MoMA's advisory board that he holds until 1941, when he resigns, criticizing the museum's failure to reflect "modern trends"[20] as well as its lack of interest in exhibiting and collecting American abstraction.

In March, Alfred Barr's historical survey "Cubism and Abstract Art" opens at the Museum of Modern Art, NY. In response to Barr's almost exclusively European exhibition, Gallatin organizes a landmark exhibition at Paul Reinhardt Galleries (NYC) entitled "The Five Contemporary American Concretionists: Biederman, Calder, Ferren, Morris and Shaw." The term "concretionist" was most likely an adaptation of the formalist term "concrete," which had originated in the 1930s with painters with Jean Hélion, Theo Van Doesburg and members of the Art Concret group. "Gallatin's show of five American Abstractionists was evidently organized as a Salon des Refusés."[21] The exhibition travels in June to Galerie Pierre in Paris and to the Mayor Gallery in London in July, with Gallatin's work replacing that of Calder's in both European exhibitions.

1937

Untitled (Cubist Architectural Abstraction), c.1935

In April, Shaw participates in the first American Abstract Artists exhibition (April 2-17) at the Squibb Gallery (745 Fifth Avenue). *The New York Times* reports: "Into the wide open spaces on the thirty-third floor of the Squibb Building. Thirty-nine American 'abstract artists' have ventured, each of them bringing examples of his own special ingenuity, each arguing in some degree his endowment as a raconteur of tales from over yonder on the Rive Gauche that have begun to assume, by this time, a sly patina of age…The show is announced as 'the first large and comprehensive demonstration of the contemporary American revolt against literary subject-paintings that have come to dominate the official and governmental art-revivals.'"[22] Shaw will participate in every annual exhibition held by the American Abstract Artists until his death in 1974.

"Frelinghuysen, Gallatin, Morris, Shaw" opens at Paul Reinhardt Galleries (NYC).

1938

Shaw attacks the "Anti-Abstractionists," arguing that the critics' objection to abstraction "would indicate that such observers have not merely failed to see abstract art but indeed any art."

In February, Shaw participates in the second American Abstract Artist Annual at the American Fine Arts Society, 215 West 57 Street. In conjunction with the exhibition, the AAA publishes an ambitious yearbook entitled *American Abstract Artists 1938*. Shaw serves on the editorial committee for the publication and provides the opening essay, "A Word to the Objector." The essay proves to be very controversial as Shaw denounces critics of abstract art. Shaw attacks the "Anti-Abstractionists" arguing that the objection critics have to abstraction "would indicate that such observers have not merely failed to *see* abstract art but indeed *any* art."[23] Ten other essays appear in the 1938 AAA yearbook, addressing various issues related to the principles and practice of abstract art.

Despite Shaw's forthrightness on social and artistic matters, according to George L.K. Morris, Shaw "declined ever to talk about himself"[24] and as friends and biographers noted Shaw was very elusive about his own life.

Shaw is invited to contribute writing to Gallatin's magazine, *Plastique* (*Plastique* 3, Spring). The issue is devoted entirely to American abstract art with articles by Gallatin ("Abstract Painting and The Museum of Living Art"), Balcomb Greene, and George L.K. Morris. Shaw's four-paragraph, one-page article, "The Plastic Polygon," provides "a lucid explanation of Shaw's most technically and professionally significant works."[25] His essay earns him a respectable reputation among the individuals and galleries interested in American abstract art.

Shaw participates in a group exhibition organized by Gallatin for Galerie Pierre in Paris (June 15-30). This is the first public exhibition of Shaw's Plastic Polygons.[26] Valentine Gallery (NYC) hosts an exhibition of new paintings by Shaw.

Shaw's *New York—Oddly Enough* (New York, Toronto: Farrar & Rinehart, Inc) is published.

In April 1937, Shaw participates in the first American Abstract Artists exhibition at the Squibb Gallery. Shaw will participate in every annual exhibition held by the American Abstract Artists until his death in 1974.

c.1939

Shaw creates designs for an exhibition of contemporary tableware at Macy's department store. Other invitees include Dr. M.F. Agha (Art Director, Condé Nast Publications), Alexander Brook (artist), Anton Bruehl (photographer), Eduard Buk-Ulreich (sculptor), William Lescaze (Architect), Mrs. Julien Levy (Julien Levy Gallery), and George Skier (designer).

1939

On January 16, a landmark exhibition of recent works by Gallatin, Morris, and Shaw opens at Jacques Seligmann & Co (NYC). *The World Telegram* announces: "Three Painters Defend Cubist Art in Joint Exhibition at Seligmann's," (January 21) the article declares "Of the three men Charles G. Shaw stands as the most original…"

The Museum of Non-Objective Painting (later renamed The Solomon R. Guggenheim Museum) opens on East 54th Street with the exhibition "Art of Tomorrow" featuring modern works of Rudolf Bauer and Vasily Kandinsky, among others. Hilla Rebay is the first director and curator.

That fall, Shaw delivered a manuscript to Margaret Wise Brown at "her 69 Bank Street Office."[27] While the editor's initial response was neither yes nor no, Ms. Brown would continue to offer Shaw encouragement and direction which "spurred Shaw on until she was at last able to accept a manuscript of his, *The Giant of Central Park*."[28] Their relationship would continue to grow professionally and socially until her death in 1952.

East Fifty Sixth Street (Coal Truck), 1946

1940

In the Spring, *The Giant of Central Park* (New York: William R. Scott, Inc.) is published. The story features a caveman-dwelling society located within Central Park. They live "on berries and fish and goat's milk and very red steak" and they are afraid of what they believe is a Giant also living in the park, but who turns out to be a young boy. The story is an interesting autobiographical sketch of Shaw as he was 6'2" and nicknamed "Big Boy" by Cole Porter, a friend since their days at Yale.

Shaw begins exhibiting regularly with the Federation of Modern Painters and Sculptors (NYC).

1941

Shaw participates in an exhibition at the Museum of Non-Objective Painting (NYC).

1942

Peggy Guggenheim opens Art of This Century, a unique gallery-museum on 57th Street, designed by Frederick Kiesler. The inaugural installation features an unconventional display of her collection. Over the next five years, the gallery mounts dozens of important exhibitions devoted to such European and American artists as Giorgio de Chirico, Robert Motherwell, Jackson Pollock, and Mark Rothko.

In December, due to wartime economy, New York University administrators decide to reclaim the space occupied by the Gallatin collection. Needing to relocate, Gallatin rebuffs overtures from Museum of Modern Art director Alfred Barr. Citing Barr's lack of sympathy for younger American abstract artists, Gallatin contacts Fiske Kimball, director of the Philadelphia Museum of Art and founder of the Art History Department at NYU. Kimball offers Gallatin a suite of rooms in which to hang his collection and agrees to allow him to continue to rotate works at will. Gallatin would eventually give the collection to the Philadelphia Museum of Art.

1944

Shaw illustrates Margaret Wise Brown's *Black and White* (New York: Harper & Bros). An odd book for its time, *Black and White* tells the story of a man "black" (not of African heritage) who lives in a black world, eating black bean soup with his black poodle. He meets a woman "white" (not of European heritage) in the form of a snowman with white rabbits and white horses. The man decides he likes the woman, and the two colors get married.

1945

Shaw begins exhibiting regularly at the Georgette Passedoit Gallery (NYC). He participates in his first of many biennials of contemporary American painting at the Whitney Museum of American Art (January). Shaw would later become a life member of the Whitney Museum.

In March, *Eight by Eight: American Abstract Painting Since 1940* an exhibition that includes work by Shaw and organized by Gallatin opens at the Philadelphia Museum of Art (PA).

Shaw starts to make assemblages, arranging early prints, dice, antique playing cards, pipes, and fabrics in shadow boxes. By the end of his life, he had created approximately 600 of these boxes, many of which decorated his apartment. These works were never exhibited publicly during his lifetime.

1947

Shaw's book *It Looked Like Spilt Milk* (New York: Harper Collins) is published. The book, directed towards early literacy, is selected by the American Institute of Graphic Arts as one of the fifty best books of the year.

1949

In February, Shaw opens a large exhibition of his work at the American British Art Center (NYC). The exhibition receives reviews from *The Sun Times*, *World-Telegram*, *Art News*, among others. *The New York Times* reports, "each canvas is both a discreet, well-mannered echo of the classic cubist balance of regularities and irregularities of shape and

Untitled (Sailboats on Blue Background),
c.1946

Shaw's early literacy book IT LOOKED LIKE SPILT MILK is selected by the American Institute of Graphic Arts as one of the fifty best books of 1947.

---

is even more certainly manifest in Mr. Shaw's New England primness and integrity of design." (February 27)

1950

Continuing as an advocate for abstraction, Shaw is quoted in the July issue of *Nouvelle Réalité*:

> "That Abstract Art stands eminently ahead of all other art to-day there can be small doubt. Perhaps this is mainly due to the fact that the public in general takes comparatively little interest in it and consequently does not influence it.
>
> To ask a painting to portray an idea is assuredly a sad perversion of the function of art. I have almost invariably found that those who object most to Abstract Art object to it for wholly non-aesthetic reason.
>
> I believe the Philistine's love of Imitation largely accounts for his apathy to all Art in general and to Abstract Art in particular."

1951

On January 23, the historic exhibition "Abstract Painting and Sculpture in America," opens at MoMA. Shaw's work is included.

On October 22, Shaw's recent work is on exhibit at the Passedoit Gallery (NYC). Fairfield Porter writes in the November issue of *ArtNews*, "Charles Shaw, for a longer time than most of his colleagues an abstract artist, is now in the midst of a new phase that might be described as cosmic naturalism." Reviewing the same exhibition, Howard Devree reports in *The New York Times*, "Shaw is a colorist who did not stand still in a realm of derivative abstraction. His currently shown canvases make use of big planes of color, overlapping of parted and recessed, with such titles as 'Flight of Time' as verbal keys to his emotionally suggestive organizations."

1952

Shaw begins writing poetry.[29]

Margaret Wise Brown dies on November 13. Upon hearing the news Shaw "grasped for breath, sounding briefly as if he might be having a heart attack."[30] Shaw would spend the

---

By 1959, Shaw has exhibited in over seventeen solo shows in New York and has contributed to more than a hundred poetry publications.

---

rest of the day "calling other friends and colleagues of hers: Bill Scott, Ursula Nordstrom, Esphyr Slobodkina [...] he wrote in his diary, 'I am more shocked and saddened than I can say...Her absence will be a large gap in my life."[31]

1954

Shaw receives his first award in poetry, the Michael Strange Poetry Award (Poetry Digest). By this time, more than 150 of his poems have appeared in numerous American and European poetry magazines. He is also a member of the Poetry Society (London), American Poets Fellowship Society, and North American Poets. He is quoted as being partial to the styles of haiku and cinquian.

1956

Construction begins on Frank Lloyd Wright's Solomon R. Guggenheim Museum (1071 Madison Avenue). The museum opens to the public on October 21, 1959, just six months after Wright's death. From the beginning, the relationship between the breathtaking architecture of the building and the art it was built to display inspires controversy and debate.

1957

Shaw begins to exhibit regularly in Nantucket (MA) at the summer home of Mrs. E. Kirk (Gladys) Haskell.

1958

Shaw receives the Nantucket Art Association Award.

1959

Into the Light (New York: The Fine Editions Press), Shaw's first book of poems is published. At this point in his career, Shaw has exhibited in over seventeen solo shows in New York and has contributed to more than a hundred poetry publications.

1960

Begins exhibiting regularly at the Art Association of Newport (RI).

1961

The complete issue of *Wisconsin Poetry Magazine* is given over to Shaw's writing.

1962

"Geometric Abstraction in America" opens at the Whitney Museum of American Art (March 20-May 13). Shaw exhibits two works: *Skyscrapers*, 1939, and *Plastic Planes*, 1945. Shaw publishes a second book of poems called *Image of Life* (New York: Poets of America Publishing).

Summer 1956, Shaw in Nantucket, Massachusetts

1963

Shaw begins to exhibit regularly at Bertha Schaefer Gallery (NYC). Paintings of this period evoke a return to early abstract themes of the 1930s, demonstrating a simplification of the image and presented on a larger format. Shaw's typical approach to making art at this time involves first creating watercolor sketches on a sketchpad (9" x 12"). Of these, Shaw would choose one to enlarge "as the basis for a small oil painting of, say, twelve-by-sixteen inches. Then, for an exhibition he would us the best of the small oils as studies for larger paintings. He was limited to the size of about five-by-seven feet, since that was the maximum-size canvas he could get into the small elevator of his apartment on East 57 Street in New York."[32]

c.1965

Shaw meets Charles C. Carpenter, an avid collector of abstract art, and like Shaw, a regular on Nantucket. It is through the encouragement of Ad Reinhardt that Carpenter seeks Shaw out. As Carpenter writes in his memoir, "Ad told me that Shaw was 'one of the pioneer abstract painters in America.'"[29] Shaw and Carpenter become fast friends: "we hit it off immediately. He was a tall, handsome man in his mid-seventies, with a dapper moustache and friendly eyes. He was a social man, a scholar, and a poet. But painting was his life [. . .] We both loved to talk art. Our talk ranged from paint quality to gossip of the art world [. . .] Charlie and I would often have lunch in his apartment [...] We ate at a small Queen Anne drop-leaf table, sitting on good American Windsor chairs, using antique pewter plates and early cutlery."[30]

1966

Shaw publishes a third book of poems *Time has No Edge* (New York: The William Frederick Press) and his paintings are featured in *Signaling Spring: Windows at Bergdorf-Goodman*, Fifth Avenue & 58th Street (NYC).

The Whitney Museum of American Art, designed by Marcel Breuer, opens on Madison Avenue (945 Madison Avenue).

1967

An exhibition of new paintings opens at New York's Century Club (NYC).

Shaw is quoted as saying that the greatest influences on his work have been "the poetry of e.e. cummings, the philosophy of George Santayana, the prose of E.M. Forster, the essays of Arthur Machen and the reflections of Alexis Carrel."[31]

1968

Shaw is named the Swordsman Free Verse Poet of the Year (September).

1973

Shaw's last one-person exhibition during his lifetime opens at Bertha Schaeffer Gallery (NYC).

1974

On April 2, Shaw dies at the age of 81. A brief obituary appears in *The New York Times* the next day. Shaw leaves the contents of his entire estate to art collector and friend Charles C. Carpenter. The contents of which includes Shaw's collection of Lewis Carroll first edition books as well as his vast collection of tarot cards, horse brasses, old English police truncheons, carved wooden tobacco figures, and scrimshaw.

"Charles Shaw's death in 1974 involved a surprise for me," wrote Charles Carpenter. "His funeral at Grace Church in New York was small, with about twenty-five people present, including George Morris and his wife Suzy Frelinghuysen, and Dorothy Miller. After the services, Shaw's lawyer came up to me and asked if I could come to her office the next day. I was aghast when I learned that Charlie had left me his entire life's art work."[32]

At the time of his death, Shaw was a member of the American Abstract Artists, the Federation of Modern Painters and Sculptors, Artist Equity Association, the Poetry Society of America, and the Poetry Society (England). He was also a Life Fellow of the International Institute of Arts and Letters. His work can be found in nearly every major museum including the Addison Gallery of American Art, Andover (MA), Art Institute of Chicago (IL), Baltimore Museum of Art (MD), Brooklyn Museum of Art (NY), Carnegie Museum of Art (PA), Cleveland Museum of Art (OH), Corcoran Gallery of Art (DC), Museum of Fine Arts, Boston (MA), Museum of Modern Art (NYC), Pennsylvania Academy of the Fine

1966, Shaw designed spring windows for the 57th Street department store Bergdorf Goodman in New York City

Arts (PA), Phillips Collection (DC), San Francisco Museum of Modern Art (CA), Smithsonian American Art Museum (DC), Wadsworth Atheneum Museum of Art (CT), Whitney Museum of American Art (NYC), and the Yale University Art Gallery (CT).

Shaw left some 50 boxes containing journals, photographs, scrapbooks, notes, sketches, among other personal items to the Archives of American Art, Washington, DC.

In the years that have followed Shaw's death, his work has continued to be included in many important museum exhibitions relating to American modernism and geometric abstraction in America. Many prominent galleries have continued to exhibit his work regularly most notably Washburn Gallery (NYC), Hirschl & Adler Galleries, Richard York Gallery (NYC), Michael Rosenfeld Gallery (NYC), among others.

NOTES

This artist chronology has been researched and written by Jason Andrew. Dating in this document for works of art and events in the artist's life reflect the most current research at the time of publication.

ENDNOTES

1. Café society was the collective description for the so-called "beautiful people" and "bright young things" who gathered in fashionable cafes and restaurants in Paris, London, Rome or New York, beginning in the late 1800s. Although members of café society were not necessarily members of The Establishment or other powerful groups, they were individuals who attended each other's private dinners and balls, took holidays in exotic locations or at elegant resorts, and whose children tended to marry the children of other café society members.
2. Buck Pennington, "The 'Floating World' in the Twenties: The Jazz Age and Charles Green Shaw." *Archives of American Art Journal*, vol. 20, no. 4 (1980), 17.
3. Quote from Bio-Press Service issued by United Press Syndicate, New York, NY. Original copy at the Charles G. Shaw Papers at The Archives of American Art, Smithsonian, Washington, DC.
4. Deems Taylor (born Joseph Taylor) (1885 - July 3, 1966) was a U.S. composer and music critic. Taylor was born in New York City and educated at New York University (NYU). He initially planned to become an architect; however, despite minimal musical training he soon took to music composition. The result was a series of works for orchestra and/or voices. In 1916, he wrote the cantata *The Chambered Nautilus*, followed by *Through the Looking-Glass* (for orchestra) in 1918, earning him public praise and recognition.
5. www.abstractamericanartists.com
6. Pennington, 18.
7. Pennington, 22.
8. A February 14, 1931 article by Shaw in the *New Yorker*, "Return to New York: after a sixteen month's absence," clearly dates Shaw's return to New York City in December of 1930, unlike previously reported by Pennington, who dates Shaw's return to America as 1932 (Pennington, 22).
9. Pennington, 23.
10. Virginia M. Mecklenburg, *The Patricia and Philip Frost Collection: American Abstraction, 1930-1945*. Exh. cat. Washington, D.C.: National Museum of American Art, 1990, 166.
11. Pennington, 23.
12. Debra Bricker Balken and Robert S. Lubar, *The Park Avenue Cubists: Gallatin, Morris, Frelinghuysen and Shaw* (New York: Grey Art Gallery, New York University, 2002), 83.
13. Ernest Boyd, "Foreword," Brochure for exhibition at Valentine Gallery, 1935, n.p.
14. Gail Stavitsky, "A Landmark Exhibition: Five Contemporary American Concretionists, March 1936," *Archives of American Art Journal*, vol. 33, no. 2 (1993), 2.
15. "Charles G. Shaw Has One Man Exhibition at New York University's Gallery of Living Art," New York University press release, April 27, 1935.
16. George L.K. Morris, "Charles Green Shaw," *The Century Yearbook: 1975* (New York: Century Association, 1975), 281.
17. Sophie Lévy, ed., *A Transatlantic Avant-Garde: American Artists in Paris, 1918-1939* (Berkeley: University of California Press, 2003), 111.
18. See Shaw's diary, vol. IV, November 22, 1935, p. 79: "To C. Biederman's (77 Wash. Place) at 10:30. Look at his canvases for about 1 ½ hours… Biederman's work is prolific, strong, and interesting. There are influences of Picasso and Miró in the main yet these canvases are also not without personality." (Shaw Papers).
19. Balken and Lubar, 70.
20. Pennington, 23.
21. Stavitsky, "A Landmark Exhibition," 3.
22. Edward Alden Jewell, "Abstract Artists open show today," *The New York Times*, April 6, 1937, 21.
23. Charles Shaw, " A Word to the Objector," *American Abstract Artists 1938*, np.
24. Balken and Lubar, 5.
25. Balken and Lubar, 70.
26. Lévy, 250.
27. Marcus, Leonard S., *Margaret Wise Brown: Awakened by the Moon*. (New York: Perennial, 2001), 118.
28. Marcus, 118.
29. Charles Shaw, "Notes on my biography 1967," Charles G. Shaw Papers Archives of American Art, Smithsonian, Washington, DC, np.
30. Marcus, 279.
31. Shaw, diary, 14 November 1952. Charles G. Shaw Papers Archives of American Art, Smithsonian, Washington, DC.
32. Charles Carpenter, *The Odyssey of a Collector* (Pittsburgh, PA: The Carnegie Museum of Art, Pittsburgh, 1996), 69.
29. Carpenter, 68.
30. Carpenter, 69.
31. Shaw, "Notes on my biography 1967."

c.1965, Charles G. Shaw

CHARLES GREEN SHAW

SELECTED PUBLIC COLLECTIONS

Addison Gallery of American Art, Phillips Academy, Andover, MA

Ackland Art Museum, University of North Carolina, Chapel Hill, NC

Akron Museum of Art, Akron, OH

Alan R. Hite Art Institute, University of Louisville, Louisville, KY

The Art Institute of Chicago, Chicago, IL

Atlanta University, Atlanta, GA

The Baltimore Museum of Art, Baltimore, MD

Berkshire Museum, Pittsfield, MA

Brooklyn Museum of Art, Brooklyn, NY

Carnegie Museum of Art, Pittsburgh, PA

Cincinnati Art Museum, Cincinnati, OH

The Cleveland Museum of Art, Cleveland, OH

Corcoran Gallery of Art, Washington, DC

The Dayton Art Institute, Dayton, OH

Denver Art Museum, Denver, CO

Fort Worth Community Arts Center, Fort Worth, TX

Georgia Museum of Art, Athens, GA

Grey Art Gallery, New York University, New York, NY

Solomon R. Guggenheim Museum of Art, New York, N

High Museum of Art, Atlanta, GA

McNay Art Museum, San Antonio, TX

Memorial Art Gallery, University of Rochester, Rochester, NY

The Metropolitan Museum of Art, New York, NY

Le Musée de l'Art Moderne, Paris, France

Museum of Fine Arts, Boston, MA

Museum of Modern Art, New York, NY

The Newark Museum, Newark, NJ

North Carolina Museum of Art, Raleigh, NC

Pennsylvania Academy of the Fine Arts, Philadelphia, PA

Philadelphia Museum of Art, Philadelphia, PA

The Phillips Collection, Washington, DC

Phoenix Art Museum, Phoenix, AZ

Rhode Island School of Design Museum, Providence, RI

Rockefeller University, New York, NY

Saint Louis Art Museum, St. Louis, MO

San Francisco Museum of Modern Art, San Francisco, CA

Sheldon Memorial Art Gallery, Lincoln, NE

Smithsonian American Art Museum, Washington, DC

Wadsworth Atheneum Museum of Art, Hartford, CT

Weatherspoon Art Museum, University of North Carolina, Greensboro, NC

Whitney Museum of American Art, New York, NY

Wichita Art Museum, Wichita, KS

Yale University Art Gallery, New Haven, CT

ONE-PERSON EXHIBITIONS

1934 "Manhattan Patterns by Charles G. Shaw," Valentine Gallery, New York, NY, April 2-April 14

1935 "Charles G. Shaw: Eight Abstract Paintings," The Gallery of Living Art, New York, NY, May 1-October 1

1938 "Charles G. Shaw," Valentine Gallery, New York, NY

1945 "Charles G. Shaw," Passediot Gallery, New York, NY, April 16-28

1946 "Recent Works by Charles G. Shaw," Passedoit Gallery, New York, NY, October 14-

1949 "Charles G. Shaw," American British Art Center, New York, NY, February 21-March 1 (catalogue)

1950 "Recent Works: Charles Shaw," Passedoit Gallery, New York, NY, September 13-October 4

1951 "Charles Shaw," Passedoit Gallery, New York, NY, October 22-November 10

1952 "Recent Works: Charles Shaw," Passedoit Gallery, New York, NY, October 13-November 1

1954 "Charles Shaw: Recent Paintings," Kenneth Taylor Galleries, August 31-September 5

"Recent Paintings: Charles Shaw," Passedoit Gallery, New York, NY, October 11-30

1956 "Charles Shaw," Passedoit Gallery, New York, NY, April 16-May 5 (exhibition brochure)

"Charles Shaw: Recent Paintings," Kenneth Taylor Galleries, July 31-August 12

1957 "Charles Shaw: Paintings" Passedoit Gallery, April 8-27 (exhibition brochure)

"Charles Shaw," E. Kirk Haskell, Nantucket, MA

1958 "Charles Shaw: Recent Oils," Passedoit Gallery, New York, NY, April 7-May 3 (exhibition brochure)

"Charles Shaw," E. Kirk Haskell, Nantucket, MA

1959 "Charles Shaw," Passedoit Gallery, March 23-April 18 (exhibition brochure)

"Charles Shaw," E. Kirk Haskell, Nantucket, MA, July 19-25

1960 "Charles G. Shaw," presented by Georgette Passedoit and Albert Landry, Albert Landry Galleries, New York, NY, March 15-April 2 (exhibition brochure)

"Charles Shaw," E. Kirk Haskell, Nantucket, MA, July 24-31

"Exhibition of Tempera Paintings by Charles Shaw," Art Association of Newport, Newport, RI, September 7-30

1961 "Charles Shaw" presented by Georgett Passedoit and Albert Landry, Albert Landry Galleries, New York, NY, April 4-24

"Recent Paintings by Charles Shaw," Theatre Workshop, Inc., New York, NY, July 23-July 29

"Charles Shaw," Southampton Art Gallery, Southampton, MA, July 13

"Charles Shaw," E. Kirk Haskell, Nantucket, MA, August

1962 "Charles Shaw," Southampton Art Gallery, Southampton, NY, July 14-July 26

"Paintings by Charles Shaw," The Art Association of Newport, Newport, RI, July 24-August 12

"Charles Shaw," E. Kirk Haskell, Nantucket, MA

1963 "Charles Shaw: Recent Paintings," Bertha Schaefer Gallery, New York, NY, January 2-26 (exhibition brochure)

"Shaw," Alan R. Hite Institute, University of Louisville, Louisville, KY, March 13-April 12 (exhibition brochure text by Carl Holty)

"Charles Shaw," E. Kirk Haskell, Nantucket, MA, August

"Shaw," Bertha Schaeffer Gallery, New York, NY, December 27-January 18, 1964 (exhibition brochure)

1964 "Paintings by Charles Shaw," Southampton Art Gallery, Southampton, NY, August 1-14

"Charles Shaw," Galerie Scott-Faure, La Jolla, CA, October 20-November 21 (exhibition brochure)

1965 "Charles Shaw," E. Kirk Haskell, Nantucket, MA

1966 "Shaw," Bertha Schaeffer Gallery, New York, NY, May 17-June 4 (exhibition brochure essay by Carl Holty)

"Recent Paintings by Charles Shaw," E. Kirk Haskell (Garden Studio Gallery), Nantucket, MA, August

1967 "Exhibition of Paintings by Centurion Charles G. Shaw," The Century Association, New York, NY, February 22-March 31

"Charles Shaw," E. Kirk Haskell, Nantucket, MA

1968 "Charles Shaw: Paintings," Bertha Schaeffer Gallery, New York, NY, October 22-November 9 (exhibition brochure)

"Recent Paintings by Charles Shaw," E. Kirk Haskell, Nantucket, MA, August 6-31

1969 "Recent Paintings by Charles Shaw," The Home of Mrs. Kirk Haskell, Nantucket, MA, August 12, 16, 21, 30

1971 "Charles Shaw," Bertha Schaeffer Gallery, New York, NY, January 26-February 13 (exhibition brochure)

1973 "Charles Shaw," Bertha Schaeffer Gallery, New York, NY, January 2-26 (exhibition brochure)

1975 "The Memorial Show of Work by Charles Green Shaw," The Century Club, New York, NY, June 3-September 29

"Charles Shaw: Works from 1935 to 1942," Washburn Gallery, New York, NY, December 2-January 10, 1976 (exhibition brochure)

1976 "Montages by Charles G. Shaw: Playing Card Collages and Boxes," Washburn Gallery, New York, NY, December 1-24

1979 "Reliefs by Charles G. Shaw: Relief Sculptures in Wood from 1937-1938," Washburn Gallery, New York, NY, January 5-February 3 (exhibition brochure)

1982 "Charles G. Shaw: Paintings from the 1930s," Washburn Gallery, New York, NY

"Charles G. Shaw: Paintings from the 1960s," Washburn Gallery, 113 Greene Street, New York, NY (exhibition brochure)

1983 "Charles G. Shaw: Playing Card Montages," Washburn Gallery, New York, NY, April 5-23 (exhibition brochure)

1985 "Charles Green Shaw: Paintings: 1930-1942," Helander Gallery, Palm Beach, FL, December 17-January 4, 1986

1987 "Charles G. Shaw: Abstractions of the Thirties," Richard York Gallery, New York, NY, May 1-30 (catalogue)

1988 "Charles G. Shaw: Biomorphic Dimensions," Washburn Gallery, New York, NY, November 1-26 (exhibition brochure)

1989 "Charles G. Shaw: Vintage Playing Card Montages," Washburn Gallery, New York, NY, December 6-January 2

1991 "Charles G. Shaw: Works from the 1930s and 1940s," Washburn Gallery, New York, NY, December 4-January 4, 1992

1997 "Charles G. Shaw," Washburn Gallery, New York, NY, January 15-February 22 (brochure)

"Charles G. Shaw," Whitney Museum of American Art, New York, NY, January 16-March 9 (brochure)

2007 "Charles G. Shaw," Michael Rosenfeld Gallery, New York, NY, November 1-December 22 (catalogue)

SELECTED GROUP EXHIBITIONS

1935 "Modern American Art in Modern Room Settings," Modernage, New York, NY, March 11-April 13

"Thirteenth Annual Spring Salon," The American Art Association, Anderson Galleries, Inc., New York, NY, May 7-May 25

"Exhibition: An American Group," Valentine Gallery, New York, NY, May 13-June 1

The Gallery of Living Art, New York University, New York, NY, November

College Art Association, New York, NY

Paul Reinhardt Galleries, New York, NY

Galerie de Paris, Paris, France

Society of Independent Artists, New York, NY

1936 "Five Contemporary American Concretionists: Biederman, Calder, Ferren, Morris, and Shaw," (curated by A.E. Gallatin) presented by The Gallery of Living Art at the Paul Reinhardt Galleries, New York, NY, March 9-31; exhibition travels to Galerie Pierre, Paris, France; Mayer Gallery, London, UK

"Salons of America," American Art Association-Anderson Galleries, New York, NY, March

Yale Club, New York, NY, March

Independent Artist's Exhibition, New York, NY

Paul Reinhardt Galleries, New York, NY

Modern Age, New York, NY

1937 "Frelinghuysen, Gallatin, Morris, Shaw," Paul Reinhardt Galleries, New York, NY, March 29-April 17

"The First Annual: American Abstract Artist Exhibition," Squibb Gallery, New York, NY, April 6-17

1938 "Oeuvres Recentes de Gallatin, Morris, Shaw," Galerie Pierre, Paris, France, June 15-30

"2nd Annual: American Abstract Artists," New York, NY; exhibition traveled (catalogue)

The Newport Art Association, Newport, RI

Shell-Mex Poster Exhibition, London, England

San Francisco Museum of Art, San Francisco, CA

1939 "Recent Paintings by Gallatin, Morris, Shaw," Jacques Seligmann & Co., New York, NY, January 16-February 8 (exhibition brochure)

"American Abstract Artists," Riverside Museum, New York, NY, March 7-26

1940 "Recent Paintings and Construction by Gallatin, Morris, Shaw," The Arts Club of Chicago, Chicago, IL, March 5-23 (exhibition brochure)

"American Abstract Art," assembled by Mr. Stephen Lion, Galerie St. Etienne, New York, NY, May 22-June 12

Museum of Non-Objective Art, New York, NY

1941 Museum of Non-Objective Art, New York, NY

1945 "Painting in the United States," Carnegie Institute, Pittsburgh, PA (SIAA)

"Eight by Eight: American Abstract Painting Since 1940," (organized by A.E. Gallatin), Philadelphia Museum of Art, Philadelphia, PA (catalogue)

"Annual Exhibition of Contemporary American Painting," Whitney Museum of American Art, November 27-January 10, 1946 (catalogue)

1947 "3rd Summer Exhibition of Contemporary Art," The State University of Iowa, Iowa City, IA, June 15-July 30 (catalogue)

"Annual Exhibition of Contemporary American Painting," Whitney Museum of American Art, New York, NY

1948 "Contemporary Illustrations of Children's Books," Worcester Art Museum, Worcester, MA, April 1-May 31 (exhibition brochure)

1948 "The Sixth Biennial Exhibition of Contemporary American Paintings," The Virginia Museum of Fine Arts, Richmond, VA, April 11-May 9 (catalogue)

1949 "13th Annual Exhibition: American Abstract Artists," Riverside Museum, New York, NY, March 29-April 17

"Salon des Realites Nouvelles," Paris, France (catalogue)

1950 "14th Exhibition of American Abstract Artists," New School for Social Research, New York, NY, March 15-31

"Salon des Realties Nouvelles," Palais des Beaux-Arts, Paris, France, June 10-July 15 (catalogue)

"Linien," Galerie Linien, Copenhagen, Denmark, August 26-September 10

1951 "Abstract Painting and Sculpture in America," Museum of Modern Art, New York, NY, January 23-March 25 (catalogue)

"15th Annual Exhibition: American Abstract Artists: Exhibition of Works of Abstract Artists of Three Nations, British, Danish, American Abstract Artists,"

Riverside Museum, New York, NY, March 12-April 1

"Exhibition of Paintings and Sculpture by Members of the New York Chapter of Artists Equity Association," Whitney Museum of American Art, New York, NY, May 28-June 10

1952 "American Abstract Artists: Sixteenth Annual," New Gallery, New York, NY, February 24-March 13

1953 "Memorial Exhibition of 17 Paintings by A.E. Gallatin and the 17th Annual Exhibition of the American Abstract Artists," Artists Equity Association, New York, NY, January 26-February 14

"Annual Exhibition of Sculpture Watercolors, Drawings," Whitney Museum of American Art, New York, NY, April 9-May 29 (catalogue)

"International Watercolor Exhibition, 17th Biennial," Brooklyn Museum, Brooklyn, NY, May 13-June 21

"Annual Spring Exhibition: Abstract American Artists," Hacker Gallery, New York, NY, May 19-June 30

1954 "18th Annual, American Abstract Artists," Riverside Museum, New York, NY, March 7-28

"Oils: by Members of the American Abstract Artists' Group," Otis Library, Otis, MA, July 8, 9

1955 "Work in Progress: Charles Shaw, Joseph Hirsch and Abraham Rattner," The Detroit Institute of Arts, Detroit, MI, January 11-February 13

"Fourteenth Annual Exhibition of The Federation," Federation of Modern Painters and Sculptors, Associated American Artists Gallery, New York, NY, February 14-26 (catalogue)

"Nebraska Art Association Sixth-Fifth Annual Exhibition," University Galleries, University of Nebraska, Lincoln, NE, February 27-March 27; exhibition traveled to Joslyn Art Museum, Omaha, NE, April 10-May 10 (catalogue)

"19th Annual, American Abstract Artists," Riverside Museum, New York, NY, February 28-March 21

"John Myers Presents: 30 Artists Equity Members," Gallery 21, New York, NY, March 15-April 2

"Gallery Highlights: Part II," Passedoit Gallery, New York, NY, September 1-24

1956 "Annual Exhibition: Paintings, Sculpture, Watercolors & Drawings," Whitney Museum of American Art, New York, NY, November 14-January 6, 1957

1957 "Peintres Americains Contemporains" Musée Galliera, Paris, France, January 24-March 5

"75 Living American Artists," an exhibition organized by the United States Committee of the International Association of Plastic Arts, Inc., sponsored by L'Association Francaise d'Action Artistique and the United States Information Agency, exhibition toured Europe including Munich and Bonn, Germany; Lille, Marseilles, Paris, Tours, Toulouse and Rouen, France

"Federation of Modern Painters and Sculptors," Chatham College, Pittsburgh, PA, January-February 12

1960 "Society for Contemporary American Art Annual Exhibition XX and 20th Anniversary Exhibit," The Art Institute of Chicago, May 17-June 18

"Collage," Gallery Mayer, New York, NY

1961 "Painting," Art at 410 Park Avenue, Chase Manhattan Bank, New York, NY, April

"International Avant-Garde Perspectives: The Americas, North & South, Europe," The Art Association of Newport, Newport, RI, July 15-30

"Collectors Choice / 2," The Saint Paul Gallery and School of Art, Saint Paul, MN, April 6-May 11

"Corcoran Gallery Biennial," Corcoran Gallery, Washington, DC

1962 "Geometric Abstraction in America," Fifth Loan Exhibition, Friends of the Whitney Museum, Whitney Museum of American Art, New York, NY, March 20-May 13 (catalogue)

"26th Annual American Abstract Artists Exhibition," IBM Gallery, New York, NY, February 5-24 (exhibition brochure)

"Selected Paintings: T. Frost, J. Girona, B. Green, W. Kamys, N. Narotzky, N. Raisen, J. Sanders, C. Shaw, Tania; Sculpture by W. Behl," Bertha Schaefer Gallery, New York, NY, May 21-June 8

1963 "22nd Annual Exhibition, Federation of Modern Painters and Sculptors," Lever House, New York, NY, January 13-27 (catalogue)

"Five Americans," Foothill College, Los Altos, CA, September

"Annual Exhibition of Contemporary American Painting," Whitney Museum of American Art, New York, NY, December 11-February 2, 1964 (catalogue)

Century Association, New York, NY

University of West Virginia, Morgantown, WV, November

State University College, Buffalo, NY, December

1964 Eastern Illinois University, Charleston, IL, January

"23rd Annual: Federation of Modern Painters and Sculptors," Lever House, New York, NY, January 12-26

Fort Wayne Museum of Art, Fort Wayne, IN, March

"Collage: Five Nationalities by Painters & Sculptors," Bertha Schaefer Gallery, New York, NY, December 1-26

"American Abstract Artists," Loeb Art Center, New York University, New York, NY

1965 "29th Annual Exhibition of Members and Guests," American Abstract Artists, Riverside Museum, New York, NY, March 14-April 25

"Federation of Modern Painters & Sculptors," Lever House, New York, NY

J. Walter Thompson Co., New York, NY

1966 "25th Annual Exhibition: Federation of Modern Painters and Sculptors," Union Carbide Corporation, New York, NY, January 11-February 1

"American Abstract Artists: 1936-1966," Riverside Museum, New York, NY

Art in the Embassies Program of United States Department of State, Washington, DC

Pennsylvania Academy of Fine Art, Philadelphia, PA

University of Colorado, Boulder, CO

1968 "Centurions Associated with the Art Students League," The Century Association, New York, NY,

February 7-March 30 (catalogue)

"HEMISFAIR '68," 1968 World's Fair, San Antonio, TX, April 6-October 6

1969 "Tenth Anniversary Exhibition: Recent Trends in American Art," The Westmoreland County Museum of Art, Greenburg, PA, May 25-July 6 (exhibition brochure)

1970 "Federation of Modern Paintings and Sculptors Exhibition," Loeb Student Center, New York University, New York, NY, December 14-January 14, 1971

1972 "American Geometric Abstraction / 1930s," Zabriskie Gallery, New York, NY, June 1-July 14

"Museum of Non-Objective Paintings," Washburn Gallery, New York, NY, December-January 1973 (exhibition brochure)

1975 "Eight by Eight," Washburn Gallery, New York, NY, October 1-26 (catalogue)

1976 "American Abstract Artists Exhibition in Honor of Josef Albers, George L.K. Morris, I. Rice Pereira, Charles Shaw," Westbeth, NY, October 2-28

1979 "c.1910-1950," Washburn Gallery, New York, NY, December 5-January 5, 1980

1980 "Meisterwerke des XX Jarhunderts, Eine Schweizer Sammlung, Moderner Kunst, 1909-1939," Kunstmuseum Winterthur, Bern, Switzerland

1983 "Beyond the Plane: Constructions in America 1930-65," New Jersey State Museum, Trenton, NJ, October 8-January 2, 1984; exhibition traveled to University of Maryland Art Gallery, January 26-March 18, 1984; Detroit Institute of Arts, April 16-June 11, 1984

"American Art of the 1930s: Selections from the Collection of the Whitney Museum," Whitney Museum of American Art, Fairfield, CT, July 8-August 31

1984 "Abstract Painting and Sculpture in America, 1927-1944," Whitney Museum of American Art, New York, NY, June 27-September 9

"Print Acquisitions: 1974-1984," Whitney Museum of American Art, New York, NY, August 29-November 25

Washburn Gallery, New York, NY, October 30-December 22

1986 "Fifty Years Ago: W.P.A./A.A.A.," Washburn Gallery, New York, NY

"A.E. Gallatin and Others," Grey Art Gallery, New York University, New York, June (catalogue)

"Modern Times: Aspects of American Art, 1907-1956," Hirschl & Adler Galleries, Inc., New York, NY, November 1-December 6 (catalogue)

1987 "Progressive Geometric Abstraction in America 1934-1955," Fred L. Emerson Gallery, Hamilton College, Clinton, NY; exhibition traveled to Mead Art Museum, Amherst College, Amherst, MA, March 31-May 1, 1988, Terra Museum of American Art, Chicago, IL, October 1- November 27, 1988; Fisher Gallery, University of Southern California, Los Angeles, CA, March-April 1989 (catalogue)

"Generations of Geometry," Whitney Museum of American Art at Equitable Center, New York, NY, June 16-August 26

1988 "New York Cubists: Works by A.E. Gallatin, George L.K. Morris, and Charles Shaw from the Thirties and Forties," Hirschl & Adler Galleries Inc., New York, NY, January 16-February 27 (catalogue)

1989 "C.1939 (New York Worlds Fair)," Washburn Gallery, New York, NY, July 1-August 31

Washburn Gallery, New York, NY, September 6-October 1

"The Patricia and Phillip Frost Collection: American Abstraction, 1930-1945," National Museum of American Art and Smithsonian Institution, Washington, DC, September 8-February 11, 1990 (publication)

1990 "In Review: Bolotowsky, Mason, Scarlett, Shaw," Washburn Gallery New York, NY, May 15-June 29 (exhibition brochure)

"American Abstract Artists," Washburn Gallery, New York, NY, September 11-October 27

"Under Five," Washburn Gallery, New York, NY, December 5-January 19, 1991

1991 "Between Mondrian and Minimalism: Neo-Plasticism in America," The Whitney Museum of American Art, Downtown at Federal Reserve Plaza, New York, NY, December 6-February 14, 1992

"The Second Wave: American Abstraction of the 1930s and 1940s, Selections from the Penny and Elton Yasuna Collection," Worcester Art Museum, Worcester, MA, September 12-December 1, 1991; exhibition traveled to the Samuel P. Harn Museum, University of Florida, Gainesville, FL, February 23-April 12, 1992; Delaware Art Museum, Wilmington, DE, October 3-November 29, 1992 (publication)

"Modern American Painting 1925-1950," Snyder Fine Art, New York, NY, September 12-October 19 (catalogue)

"Circle and Square: Geometric Abstraction and Constructivism in the Americas, 1934-1950," Kouros Gallery, New York, NY

1992 "Gifts and Acquisitions in Context," Whitney Museum of American Art, New York, NY, May 22-September 20

"Parallel Vision," Whitney Museum of American Art, New York, NY, July 31-October 25

"The Geometric Tradition in American Art, 1930-90," Whitney Museum of American Art, New York, NY, December 9-February 14, 1993

"Fables, Fantasies and Everyday Things," Whitney Museum of American Art, New York, NY, November 20-January 31, 1993

1993 "The Uses of Geometry: Then and Now" Snyder Fine Art, New York, NY, October 29-December 4 (catalogue)

"Aspects of American Abstraction, 1930-1942," Michael Rosenfeld Gallery, New York, NY, February 11-March 27 (catalogue)

1994 "Counterpoints: American Art, 1930-1945," Michael Rosenfeld Gallery, New York, NY, April 7-June 4 (catalogue)

"Top Flight: Group Show," Washburn Gallery, New York, NY, September 1-20

1995 "1937 - American Abstract Art," Snyder Fine Art, New York, NY, September-October (catalogue)

1996 "Charles H. Carpenter, Jr: The Odyssey of a Collector," Carnegie Museum of Art, Pittsburgh, PA, March 23-June 9; exhibition traveled to Whitney Museum of American Art, New York, NY, January 16-March 9, 1997 (publication)

"Abstraction Across America, 1934-1946," Michael Rosenfeld Gallery, New York, NY, September 11-November 9 (catalogue)

1998 "Defining the Edge: Early American Abstraction, Selections from the Collection of Dr. Peter B. Fischer," Laguna Art Museum, Laguna Beach, CA, January 10-March 15; exhibition traveled to Michael Rosenfeld Gallery, New York, NY, March 26-May 30 (catalogue)

"American Abstract Art of the 1930s and 1940s: The J. Donald Nichols Collection," Wake Forest University Fine Arts Gallery, Wake Forest University, Winston-Salem, NC, August 28-October 11 (publication)

2001 "Modern American Art of the 1930s and 40s," Gary Snyder Fine Art, New York, NY, June 1-August 2

2002 "Austere Geometry (1955-1975) & Modern American Masterworks (1930-1945)," Gary Snyder Fine Art, New York, NY, September 13-October 26

"Early American Abstraction: Small Scale, Large Dimension," Michael Rosenfeld Gallery, New York, NY, November 7-January 11, 2003 (catalogue)

"New York Abstraction 1930-1945," Gary Snyder Fine Art, New York, NY, December 12-January 25, 2003

2003 "The Park Avenue Cubists: Gallatin, Morris, Frelinghuysen and Shaw," The Grey Art Gallery, New York University, New York, NY, January 14-March 29; exhibition traveled to The Addison Gallery of American Art, Phillips Academy, Andover, MA, April 22-July 31 (publication)

"The 1940s: Modern American Art & Design," Michael Rosenfeld Gallery, New York, NY, September 9-November 1 (catalogue)

"The Transatlantic Avant-Garde: American Artists in Paris, 1918-1939," Musee d'Art Americain, Giverny, France, August 31-November 30; exhibition traveled to Tacoma Art Museum, Tacoma, WA, December 18-March 28, 2004; Terra Museum of American Art, Chicago, IL, April 17-June 27, 2004 (publication)

"Modern American Art 1930-1975," Gary Snyder Fine Art, New York, NY, October 31-December 20

2004 "The 1930s: Modern American Art & Design," Michael Rosenfeld Gallery, New York, NY, September 10-October 30 (catalogue)

"Breaking Boundaries: Early American Abstraction, 1930-1945," Michael Rosenfeld Gallery, New York, NY, September 10-October 30

2005 "Evolution in Abstraction: Antecedents and Descendents," D. Wigmore Fine Art, Inc., April 15-May 31 (catalogue)

2006 "Geometric Abstraction: Two Generations," D. Wigmore Fine Art, Inc, February 15-May 15 (catalogue)

81

1920-1929	"Latest Works of Fiction: Society Fun: Heart In a Hurricane." *The New York Times*, March 27, 1927: 14, 19

1930-1935	"In Current Art Magazines." *The New York Times*, March 11, 1934: X12

"Charles G. Shaw." (Valentine Gallery) *The Sun*, March 31, 1934

"Variety of Art on Calendar." (Charles G. Shaw at Valentine) *The New York Times*, April 2, 1934: 15

Genauer, Emily. "Memorial Show of Daingerfield: Late Artists' Work Seen at Gallery." *New York Telegram*, April 5, 1934

McBride, Henry. "Charles G. Shaw at Valentine." *New York Sun*, April 7, 1934

"Manhattan Patterns at Valentine Gallery." *Art News*, April 7, 1934

"Exhibit of City Scenes: Chas G. Shaw's Work at Valentine's." *New York Evening Post*, April 7, 1934

"Exhibition of the Week." (Valentine Gallery) *New York American*, April 7, 1934

Devree, Howard. "A Reviewer's Note Book." (Shaw at Valentine) *New York Times*, April 8, 1934: X7

"New York Designs By Charles Shaw." *New York Herald Tribune*, April 8, 1934

Winchell, Walter. "Lesson in Painting." (Valentine Gallery) *Daily Mirror*, April 10, 1934

"Shaw's Manhattan Patterns." *The Wall Street Journal*, April 11, 1934

Godsoe, Robert Ulrich. "The Art Marts." (Valentine Gallery) *New York Herald Tribune*, April 12, 1934

"Lesson in Painting." (Valentine Gallery) *Evening Tennessean*, April 13, 1934

"Manhattan Patterns." *New Yorker Magazine*, April 14, 1934

Art Listing. *Art News*, April 14, 1934

Mumford, Lewis. "The Art Galleries: Memorials and Moderns." *New Yorker Magazine*, April 14, 1934

"Around the Galleries." *New York Telegraph*, April 15, 1934

"Shaw Presents Something New." (Valentine Gallery) *Art Digest*, April 15, 1934

"Charles G. Shaw at Valentine." *New York Telegraph*, April 22, 1934

McIntyre, O. O. "New York Day by Day." *New York American*, May 9, 1934

Sompayrac, Irma de B. "Art in Town." *Park Avenue Social Review*, May 1934

Art Listing. *New Yorker Magazine*, March, 1935

"Attractions in the Galleries." (Modernage) *New York Sun*, March 1935

Keller, Allan. "Park Ave. Artists in Show of the Independents May Turn Old Familiar Reds into Pastel Pink." *New York World-Telegram*, March 30, 1935

McBride, Henry. "Politics and Art Expression: Exhibition of Independent Society Riotous and Incoherent." *New York Sun*, April 13, 1935

"Calendar of Exhibitions in New York." *Art News*, April 27, 1935

"School Post Box: One-Man Exhibition." *New York Evening Post*, April 27, 1935

"The Gallery of Living Art." *The Sun*, April 27, 1935

"The Gallery of Living Art." *World Telegram*, April 27, 1935

"News of the Art World." (Gallery of Living Art) *The New York Times*, April 28, 1935: X7

Jewell, Edward Alden. "Three Shows Here of Abstract Art." (The Gallery of Living Art) *The New York Times*, May 3, 1935: 22

Jewell, Edward Alden. "In the Realm of Art: From the Literal to the Abstract." *The New York Times*, May 5, 1935: X7

"One Man Shatters Rule." *Literary Digest*, May 11, 1935

McBride, Henry. "The Salons of America." *New York Sun Times*, May 11, 1935: 29

Art Listing. *New Yorker Magazine*, May 11, 1935

"Poor Paintings Mar Week's Art Exhibits." *New York World-Telegram*, May 11, 1935

"Art Notes: Charles G. Shaw at The Gallery of Living Art." *New York Herald Tribune*, May 12, 1935

Jewell, Edward Alden. "New Group Shows for American Art." *The New York Times*, May 14, 1935: 19

"Attractions in the Galleries." (American Exhibition at Valentine Gallery) *The New York Sun Times*, May 18, 1935

Breuning, Margaret. "Group Shows: New Work and New Artists in Week's Exhibitions." (Gallery of Living Art), *New York Post*, May 18, 1935

"Summer Exhibits Underway: One of the Most Rewarding Shows is That of 'American Group' at the

Valentine Galleries." *New York World-Telegram*, May 18, 1935

"American Group at Valentine." *The New York Times*, May 19, 1935

Godsoe, Robert Ulrich. "The Art Marts." *North Shore News*, May 23, 1935

"Exhibit Distinctive." *American Business Survey*, June 1935

Jewell, Edward Alden. "Charles Shaw at A. E. Gallatin's Gallery of Living Art." *The New York Times*, June 2, 1935: X7

"Shaw abstractions on view." *Eagle*, June 2, 1935

Art Listing. *Villager*, June 13, 1935

Town & Country, August 1935

"Koch Work Outstanding in First Fall Group Show." *New York World-Telegram*, September 14, 1935

"In the Local Spotlight." (Valentine Gallery) *The New York Times*, September 15, 1935: X7

Jewell, Edward Alden. "Bearding the 'Abstract': Exploring Some Highways and Byways of An Elusive and Loosely Used Term." *The New York Times*, September 22, 1935: X10

"Attractions in the Galleries." *The Sun*, November 2, 1935

Jewell, Edward Alden. "Also These: In Local Galleries and at Museums." *The New York Times*, November 3, 1935: X9

"N.Y.U. Acquired Modern Works." *American Art News*, November 16, 1935

1936-1939

"Artists to Exhibit at N.Y.U. Gallery." *American*, February 24, 1936

Town & Country, March 1936

"American Abstractionists." *Art Digest*, March 1, 1936

"Art of many Lands in Current Shows: Five American 'Concretionists' Exhibit Through Gallery of Living Art." *The New York Times*, March 9, 1936

McBride, Henry. "America Also Goes Abstract: Five 'Concretionists' in Session at the Reinhardt Galleries." *The Sun*, March 14, 1936

"Two Exhibits Anti-Climax Abstracts." *New York World-Telegram*, March 14, 1936

"Concretionists' Called Tasteful in Their Exhibit." *New York Post*, March 14, 1936: 22

Simonton, Thomas. "Various Galleries Show Abstract Art; Other Exhibitions." *New York American*, March 14, 1936

Jewell, Edward Alden. "The Realm of The Left: New Outbreaks of Abstraction Continue Inventory of a Phase of Modernism." *The New York Times*, March 15, 1936: X8

"More From The Modernists." *New York Herald-Tribune*, March 15, 1936

"Gallery of Living Art." *Eagle*, March 15, 1936

"Abstract Art Revives." *San Francisco News*, March 18, 1936

"Art Brevities." *The New York Times*, March 21, 1936: 15

"Shaw, Calder and Other Concertionists." *Art News*, March 21, 1936

Brewer, Ann. The Art of University Men: Painting and Sculpture at the Yale Club." *Art News*, March 28, 1936

McCausland, Elizabeth. "Gallery Notes." *Parnassus* (April 1936): 28

"Spring Show Opened By Salons of America." *New York Herald Tribune*, May 6, 1936

"At Reinhardt Galleries." *New York Sun*, April 3, 1937

"Abstract Americans." *New York American*, April 3, 1937

"Reinhardt Galleries." *Evening Post*, April 3, 1937

"Reinhardt Galleries." *New York Herald Tribune*, April 4, 1937

Jewell, Edward Alden. "Abstract Artist Open Show Today: Gertrude Greene, Charles Shaw and George Morris Among 39 Represented." *The New York Times*, April 6, 1937: 21

McCausland, Elizabeth. "Gallery Notes." *Parnassus* 10, no. 2 (February 1938): 27-29

Jewell, Edward Alden. "The Man and The Artist." *The New York Times*, February 20, 1938: 155

"Three Painters Defend Cubist Art in Joint Exhibition at Seligmann's." *World Telegram*, January 21, 1939

D.B. "Three Native Abstactionists: A.E. Gallatin, Morris, Shaw." *Art News* (January 28, 1939)

Pictures on Exhibit (February 1939)

"The Abstract Trio." *Art Digest*, February 1, 1939

What's On About Town, *New Yorker Magazine*, February 4, 1939

"Heard at the Galleries." *Pictures on Exhibit* (June 1939)

1940-1949	

"Modern Milestones in Sculpture." *Art News* (February 1941)

Johnson, Rhodes. "In Defense of Abstract Art." *Parnassus* 12, no. 8 (December 1940): 6-10

Greenberg, Clement. "Art Chronicle: The Decline of Cubism." *Partisan Review* XV (March 1948): 366-369

"Highly Modern: Painting by C.G. Shaw, Sculpture by Robus." *The New York Times*, Sunday, February 27, 1949: X8

Genauer, Emily. "This Week in Art: Shaw's Handsome Abstractions Show Style and Taste." *The World Telegram*, Monday, February 28, 1949

S.P. "Charles Shaw." (American British) *Art News* (February 1949)

M.L. "Strength and Wit of Shaw." (American British Art Center) *Art Digest* 23, no. 11 (March 1, 1949)

"American British Art Center." *Sun Times*, Saturday, February 1949

P.V.B. 'The Abstract Paintings of Charles G. Shaw." *New York Herald Tribune*, February 1949

Burrows, Carlyle. "Thirteenth Show by Abstract Artists Is Open at the Riverside Museum." *New York Herald Tribune*, March 29, 1949

Coates, Robert M. "The Art Galleries: George Braque, and the American Abstract Artists." *New Yorker Magazine*, April 9, 1949

Sharp, Marynell. "Abstract Annual." *Art Digest*, April 15, 1949

Hess, Thomas B. "The Abstract Artists'." *Art News* (May 1949)

Krasne, Belle. "Modern Federation in 9th Annual Show." *Art Digest*, October 15, 1949

1950-1959	

"American Abstract Artists at New School." *The New York Times*, 1950

Cover Illustration. *La Revue Moderne des Arts et de La Vie*, Paris, France, February 1950

Clochettes, G. Des. "Charles G. Shaw." *La Revue Moderne*, February 1950

Nouvelles Realities, July 1950

M.B. "Charles Shaw." *Art Digest*, September 15, 1950

"Making a return appearance with new paintings, Charles G. Shaw." *New York Herald Tribune*, September 17, 1950

"Strength: A painting by Charles G. Shaw." (Passedoit) *The New York Times*, September 17, 1950

B.H. "Charles Shaw." (Passedoit) *Art News,* vol. 49, no. 6 (October 1950)

Kreider, Stanton. "American Abstract Artists: Their Fifteenth Anniversary Show Includes Some Europeans." *Pictures on Exhibit* (April 1951)

E.G. "Art Exhibition Notes." (Passedoit) *New York Herald Tribune*, Friday, October 26, 1951

Kreider, Stanton. "Gallery Preview." *Pictures on Exhibit* (November 1951)

J.F. "Charles Shaw." *Art Digest* (November 1951)

Porter, Fairfield. "Charles Shaw." *Art News*, vol. 50, no. 7 (November 1951)

Devree, Howard. 'New Artists' Work in Week's Openings." (Passedoit) *The New York Times*, October 22, 1951: 17

Devree, Howard. "Idiom or Formula." *The New York Times*, October 1951

E.C.M. "Charles Shaw." (Passedoit) *Art News* (October 1952)

"Charles Shaw." *Pictures on Exhibit* (October 1952)

J.F. "Charles Shaw." (Passedoit) *Art Digest* (October 15, 1952)

Burrows, Carlyle. "Dynamic Abstraction." (Passedoit) *New York Herald Tribune*, Sunday, October 19, 1952

Devree, Howard. "Personal Abstraction." (Passedoit) *The New York Times*, Sunday, October 19, 1952

Geist, Sidney. "Whitney Annual: Confusion of Issues." *Art Digest* 27, no. 15 (May 1, 1953)

Kreider, Stanton. "Gallery Previews in New York." *Pictures on Exhibit* (June 1953)

B. H. "American Abstract Artists." (Hacker) *Art News* (June 1953)

Sutherland, Sandy. "Three Artists to Exhibit At Taylor Galleries." *Inquirer and Mirror*, August 28, 1954

Faison, S. Lane, Jr. "Charles Shaw." (Passedoit) Publication unknown (1954)

Porter, Fairfield. "Charles Shaw." (Passedoit Gallery) *Art News*, vol. 53, no. 6 (October 1954)

Devree, Howard. "About Art and Artists: Charles Shaw's Paintings at the Passedoit Use Color to Set a Psychological Mood." *The New York Times*, Tuesday, October 12, 1954

Burrows, Carlyle. "Abstract Transitions." (Passedoit Gallery) *New York Herald Tribune*, October 17, 1954

Charles G. Shaw." (Passedoit Gallery) *The New York Times*, Sunday, October 24, 1954

"Charles Shaw." (Passedoit Gallery) *Art Digest*, November 1, 1954

"Forty Artist Equity Members at Gallery 21." *Pictures on Exhibit*, March 1955

R.R. "Artists Equity Group." *Arts Digest*, April 1955

Burrows, Carlyle. "A Gallery Tour in June." (Passedoit Gallery) *New York Herald-Tribune*, June 12, 1955

Devree, Howard. "Current Group Shows." *The New York Times*, June 19, 1955

S.B. "Group Show." (Passedoit) *Arts Digest*, September 15, 1955

S.K. "Gallery Previews in New York." *Pictures on Exhibition* (December 1955)

L.G. "Charles Shaw." *Arts Magazine* (April 1956)

"New Shaw Abstracts." *New York Herald-Tribune*, April 21, 1956

Art Listing. *New Yorker Magazine*, April 18, 1956

E.C.M. "Charles Shaw." *Art News* (May 1956)

McNeil, George. "American abstractionists venerable at twenty." *Art News* (May 1956)

"People in the Arts." *Arts Magazine* (May 1956)

"Charles G. Shaw." *Yale Alumni Magazine*, June 1956

"Artists at Passedoit." *New York Herald-Tribune*, June 17, 1956

Art Listing. *New Yorker Magazine*, July 1956

Burrows, Carlyle. "Art: American." *New York Herald-Tribune*, November 1, 1956

Genauer, Emily. "Nature or a Style." *New York Herald-Tribune*, November 18, 1956

Devree, Howard. "Contemporary Work at the Whitney and National Academy-Vytlacil." *The New York Times*, November 18, 1956

M.S. "Federation of Modern Painters and Sculptors." *Arts Magazine* (December 1956)

E.P. "Charles Shaw." *Arts Magazine* (April 1957)

Jena, Jenette. "Paintings at Chatham 'Modern' in Philosophy." *American Federation of Arts Letter*, April 1957

"New Work by Shaw." *New York Herald-Tribune*, April 13, 1957

Devree, Howard. "Chiefly Americans: A Water-Color Survey." *The New York Times*, April 14, 1957

Devree, Howard. "In Veins of Today: Two Group Exhibitions Vital and Varied." *The New York Times*, March 17, 1957: X11

V.Y. "Trends in Watercolors Today, Italy and US." (Brooklyn Museum of Art) *Arts Magazine* (May 1957)

Campbell, Lawrence. "Trends in watercolor today." (Brooklyn Museum of Art) *Art News* (May 1957)

"Charles Shaw." (Haskell) *Nantucket Inquirer*, August 1957

Preston, Stuart. "A Renoir Galaxy-Exhibitions of the Week." (Passedoit Gallery) *The New York Times*, April 13, 1958: X10

Gensuer, E. "Cloud-Shapes by Shaw." New York Herald-Tribune, April 1958

Campbell, Lawrence. "Charles Shaw." *Art News*, May 1958

M.S. "Charles Shaw." *Arts Magazine*, May 1958

C. Z. O. "Charles Shaw." *Pictures on Exhibit*, May 1958

Art Listing. *New Yorker Magazine*, May 1958

"Charles G. Shaw." *Yale Alumni Magazine*, June 1958

Preston, Stuart. "Curtain Calls of '57-58." *The New York Times*, June 1, 1958

"Charles G. Shaw." *Yale Alumni Magazine*, July 1958

Campbell, Lawrence. "Reviews and Previews: Charles Shaw." (Passedoit) *Art News*, vol. 58, no. 1 (March 1959): 15

"Charles Shaw." *Pictures on Exhibit*, March 1959

Devree, Howard. "In Abstract View: Work by British and American Artists." *The New York Times*, March 29, 1959: X13

Burrows, Carlyle. "Art Exhibition Notes: Charles Shaw Show." *New York Herald-Tribune*, March 28, 1959

Breuning, Margaret. "Charles Shaw." *Arts Magazine*, April 1959

Art Listing. *New Yorker Magazine*, April 4, 1959

"Charles G. Shaw." *Yale Alumni Magazine*, May 1959

Preston, Stuart. "Art: Bank Shows Interest in Design." *The New York Times*, October 24, 1959: 18

Sandler, Irving H. "Reviews and Previews: Charles Shaw." (Landry) *Art News*, vol. 59, no. 1 (March 1960): 13

"Charles Shaw." *Yale Alumni Magazine*, March 1960

G.S. "Charles Shaw." (Albert Landry) *Pictures on Exhibit*, March 1960

Preston, Stuart. "Artist's Attitudes." *The New York Times*, March 20, 1960: X20

"Footnotes on Gallery Tour." *New York Herald-Tribune*, March 20, 1960

"Charles Shaw." *Yale Alumni Magazine*, June 1960

"Private Exhibition of Paintings." *Inquirer & Mirror*, July 22, 1960

"Charles Shaw's Paintings on Exhibition." *Inquirer & Mirror*, July 23, 1960

"Shaw, Chapin Exhibits Will Highlight Summer." *Vineyard Gazette*, August 19, 1960

"Shaw Abstracts on Exhibition At Art Assn." *New Port Daily News*, Thursday, September 8, 1960: 2

Preston, Stuart. "Art: Display of Collages." (Gallery Mayer) *The New York Times*, September 24, 1960: 27

Karr, Peter. "Nantucket Art World." *Nantucket Town Crier*, July, 28, 1961

"Preview of Benefit Art Show Fri Eve." *Southampton Press*, July 13, 1961

J.K. "Charles Shaw" *Art News*, April 1961

J.T. "Charles Shaw" *Pictures on Exhibit*, April 1961

Art Listing. *New York Herald Tribune* April 9, 1961

Art Listing. *The New York Times*, April 23, 1961

Art Listing. *New Yorker Magazine*, May 18, 1962

Art Listing. *Yale Alumni Magazine*, December 1962

Art Listing. *Town & Country*, July 1962

Art Listing. *Nantucket Inquirer and Mirror*, August 3, 1962

Art Listing. *Nantucket Inquirer and Mirror*, August 10, 1962

"News Items…" *The Creative Person*, April 1961

"Shaw's Paintings to be Shown." *Newport, RI Daily News*, July 21, 1962: 2

"Shaw Show." *The Writer's Voice*, April 1961

Preston, Stuart. "Art." *The New York Times*, February 11, 1962

"Charles Shaw." (Schaefer) *New York Visitor's Review*, January 1963

D.A. "Paintings by Shaw" *The Christian Science Monitor*, January 1963

S.C.F. "Charles Shaw" *Art News*, January 1963

S.T. "Charles Shaw." (Schaefer) *Arts Magazine* (February 1963)

van der Hoeven, Gay. "Shaw at Schaefer" *Manhattan East*, January 10, 1963

Preston, Stuart. "Artists Are Busy with Exhibitions" *The New York Times*, January 7, 1963

Preston, Stuart. "Catch '63 So Far: Winter's Outstanding Shows Surveyed." *The New York Times*, April 7, 1963

Preston, Stuart. "Package Deals: Group Exhibitions of Contemporary Art." *The New York Times*, July 7, 1963: X8

"Charles Shaw Exhibit." *Nantucket Inquirer & Mirror*, August 1, 1963

Spitzer, Fritz. "The Nantucket Art World." *Nantucket Town Crier*, August 1, 1963

Price, Margaret. "The Artist On Nantucket." *Nantucket Inquirer & Mirror*, August 8, 1963

O'Doherty, Brian. "Apart From Group Shows, Galleries Are Bare—Shaw Abstractions on Display." *The New York Times*, December 28, 1963: 20

F.T.R. "Charles Shaw." *Pictures on Exhibit* (January 1964)

Art Listing. *Time Magazine* (January 1964)

J.H.B. "Charles Shaw." *Art News* (January 1964)

"Shaw at Schaefer." *Manhattan East*, January 2, 1964

Gruen, John. "How to Fail Through Success." *New York Herald-Tribune*, January 12, 1964

Judd, Donald. "Charles Shaw." *Arts Magazine* (February 1964)

"Charles G. Shaw." *Yale Alumni Magazine*, March 1964

"Southampton Art Gallery to Exhibit Chas Shaw Works." *Southampton Press*, July 30, 1964

"Southampton Art Gallery." *The Hamptons Weekly*, July 30, 1964

"Charles Shaw." *Time*, June 3 1965

J.S. "Charles Shaw." *Pictures on Exhibit*

N.E. "Charles Shaw." *Art News*, Spring 1965

Siple, Molly. "Shaw at Schaefer" *Park East*

"Charles G. Shaw." *Yale Alumni Magazine*, July 1966

"Charles G. Shaw." *Yale Alumni Magazine*, December 1966

"Charles G. Shaw." *Yale Alumni Magazine*, April 1967

Carpenter, Charles H. "Charles Shaw's 17th one-man show here." *Inquirer & Mirror*, August 14, 1968

R.S. "Charles Shaw." *Arts*, 1968

S.A.K. "Charles Shaw." *Art News* (Fall 1968)

"Charles G. Shaw." *Yale Alumni Magazine*, May-December 1968

"Charles Shaw Exhibition." *Inquirer & Mirror*, August 1, 1968

"Charles G. Shaw." *Yale Alumni Magazine*, December 1969

1970-1979

McCoy, Garnett. "Artists and Writers in America." *Archives of American Art Journal*, vol. 16, no. 4 (1976): 2-15

Morris, George L.K. "Charles Shaw." *Century Yearbook*, New York: Century Association, 1975

Russell, John. "Art: The American Idiom of Charles Shaw." *The New York Times*, January 3, 1976

Larsen, Susan. "The American Abstract Artists: A Documentary History." *Archives of American Art Journal*, vol. 14, no. 1 (1974): 2-7

Larsen, Susan. "Through the Looking Glass with Charles Green Shaw." *Arts Magazine*, vol. 51, no. 4 (December 1976): 82

Larsen, Susan. "Albert Gallatin: The Park Avenue Cubist Who went Downtown." *Art News* LXXVII (Dec. 1978): 80-84

1980-1989

Pennington, Buck. "The 'Floating World' in the twenties: The Jazz Age and Charles Green Shaw." *Archives of American Art Journal 20*, no. 4 (1980): 17-24

Kramer, Hilton. "Charles Shaw- In the Minimal Tradition." *The New York Times*, February 21, 1982: A 25

Carpenter, C. "Charles Shaw." *Art International*, 25 (November/December 1982): 20-22

Russell, John. "Heroic Sublime." *The New York Times*, June 13, 1986: C32

Smith, Roberta. "Charles Shaw." (Richard York Gallery) *The New York Times*, May 8, 1987: C27

1990-1999

Stavitsky, Gail. "Landmark Exhibition: Five Contemporary American Concretionists." *Archives of American Art Journal*, vol. 33, no. 2 (1993): 2-10.

Berman, Avis. "American Modernisms (October) and Editors, "In the Galleries." *Art & Auction* (September 1995)

Cotter, Holland. "Charles G. Shaw." (Washburn) *The New York Times*, January 31, 1997: C28

Kramer, Hilton. "Painter of Privilege." *Art & Antiques*. April 1997

2000-PRESENT

Glueck, Grace. "Cubists Living in Luxury, Not Bohemian Garrets." *The New York Times*, January 24, 2003: F1

Kimball, Roger. "The Park Avenue Cubists: Gallatin, Morris, Frelinghuysen and Shaw at the Grey Art Gallery" *The New Criterion*, 21, no. 6, Fall 2003

Kramer, Hilton. "Saluting Pioneer Abstractionists." *Art & Antiques*, March 2003

Temin, Christine. "Park Avenue Cubists Share Gallery Spotlight." *The Boston Globe*, June 11, 2003: F1

SELECTED EXHIBITION CATALOGUES

New York, NY. *American Abstract Artists*. Essays by Charles G. Shaw, Albert Swinden, George L. K. Morris, Harry Holtzman, Ibram Lassaw, Balcomb Greene, and others, 1938.

The American British Art Center, New York, NY. *Charles G. Shaw*. 1949.

Whitney Museum of American Art, New York, NY. *Annual Exhibition of Contemporary American Painting*. 1945.

Philadelphia Museum of Art, Philadelphia, PA. *Eight by Eight: American Abstract Painting Since 1940*. 1945

Palais des Beaux-Arts, Paris, France. *Salon des Realties Nouvelles*. 1950.

The Museum of Modern Art, New York, NY. *Abstract Painting and Sculpture in America*. 1951

Whitney Museum of American Art, New York, NY. *Geometric Abstraction in America*. 1962.

Whitney Museum of American Art, New York, NY. *Annual Exhibition of Contemporary American Painting*. 1964

Washburn Gallery, New York, NY. *Charles G. Shaw: Paintings from the 1930s. 42 East 58/ Paintings from the 1960s, 113, Greene*. 1982.

Whitney Museum of American Art, New York, NY. *Abstract Painting and Sculpture in America, 1927-1944*. 1983.

Hirschl & Adler Galleries, Inc. New York, NY. *Modern Times: Aspects of American Art, 1907-1956*. Introduction by Douglas Dreishpoon, 1986.

Fred L. Emerson Gallery, Hamilton College, Clinton, NY. *Progressive Geometric Abstraction in America 1934-1955*.

Essays by Harry Holtzman and Susan C. Larsen, 1987.

Richard York Gallery, New York, NY. *Charles Shaw: Abstractions of the Thirties*. 1987.

Hirschl & Adler Galleries, Inc. New York, NY. *New York Cubists: Works by A.E. Gallatin, George L.K. Morris, and Charles Shaw from the Thirties and Forties*. Essay by Douglas Dreishpoon, 1988

The Whitney Museum of American Art, New York, NY. *Charles G. Shaw: Collection in Context*. Essay by Beth Venn, 1997

SELECTED PUBLICATIONS

American Abstract Art of the 1930s and 1940s: The J. Donald Nichols Collection. Winston Salem: Wake Forest University, 1998.

Auping, Michael. Abstraction Geometry Painting: Selected Geometric Abstract Painting in America Since 1945. New York: Albright-Knox Art Gallery, 1989.

Balken, Debra and Robert S. Lubar. The Park Avenue Cubists: Gallatin, Morris, Frelinghuysen and Shaw. New York: The Grey Art Gallery, 2002.

Bearden, Romare and Carl Holty. A Painter's Mind: A Study of the Relations of Structure and Space. New York: Crown, 1969.

Carter, Richard, ed. The Patricia and Phillip Frost Collection: American Abstraction, 1930-1945. Washington DC: National Museum of American Art and Smithsonian Institution, 1989.

Carpenter, Charles H. The Odyssey of a Collector. Pittsburgh, PA: The Carnegie Museum of Art, 1996.

Lane, John C. and Susan Larsen, eds. Abstract Painting and Sculpture in America 1927-1944. Pittsburgh: Carnegie Institute in association with Harry N. Abrams, Inc, 1983.

Levy, Sophie, ed. A Transatlantic Avant-Garde: American Artists in Paris, 1918-1939. University of California Press: Berkeley, Los Angeles, 2003.

Mecklenburg, Virginia M. The Patricia and Phillip Frost Collection Catalogue: American Abstraction 1930-1945. Washington DC: Smithsonian, 1989.

Strickler, Susan E. and Gustafson, Elaine D. The Second Wave: American Abstraction of the 1930s and 1940s: Selections from the Penny and Elton Yasuna Collection. Worcester: The Worcester Museum of Art, 1981.

CHARLES SHAW AS AN EDITOR

Yale Literary Magazine, 1927-28

The Miscellany, 1929-1931

Museum of Modern Art Bulletin, 1935-36

Partisan Review, 1937

Plastique, 1937

CHARLES SHAW AS ILLUSTRATOR

Baruchy, Dorothy. *Pitter Patter*. New York: William R. Scott, Inc., 1943

Brown, Margaret Wise. *Black and White*. New York: William R. Scott, Inc., 1944

Scott, William R. *This Is the Milk That Jack Drank*, (adapted from Mother Goose) New York: William R Scott, 1943

Brown, Margaret Wise. *The Winter Noisy Book*. New York: Harper Collins, 1947

Scott, William R. *The Apple That Jack Ate*. New York: William R. Scott, Inc., 1951

Booth, Philip. *Beyond Our Fears*. New York: St. George's Episcopal Church, 1969

McCullough, John G. *Dark is Dark*, 1947

PUBLISHED WRITINGS BY CHARLES SHAW

Shaw, Charles G. *Heart in a Hurricane*. New York: Brentano's, 1927

Shaw, Charles G. *The Low Down*. New York: Holt, 1928

Shaw, Charles G. *Night Life: Vanity Fair's Intimate Guide to New York After Dark*. New York: The John Day Company, 1930

Shaw, Charles G. *Lady by Chance*. New York: McCaulay, 1932

Shaw, Charles G. *New York- Oddly Enough*. New York: Farrar and Reinhart, Inc., 1938

Shaw, Charles G. *The Giant of Central Park*. New York: William R. Scott, Inc., 1940

Shaw, Charles G. *The Blue Guess Book: A Young Riddle Book in Pictures*, New York: William R. Scott, Inc., 1942

Shaw, Charles G. *It Looked Like Spilt Milk*. New York: Harper Collins, 1947

Shaw, Charles, "Before Kings and Queens Had Two Heads." *Connoisseur* 127, no. 524 [January 1952]: 162-166, 201

Shaw, Charles G. "The Very Now." The Phylon Quarterly, vol. 18, no. 2 (2nd Quarter, 1957): 161.

Shaw, Charles G. *Into the Light*. New York: Fine Editions Press, 1959

Shaw, Charles G. *Image of Life*. New York: Poets of America Publishing, 1962

Shaw, Charles G. *Time Has No Edge* (A Poetry Collection). New York: Frederick-William, 1966.

Shaw, Charles G. *Toward Tomorrow*. Tremont, Ill.: Strato-Jet Poets, 1971.

AWARDS & HONORS

1960	Off-Island Show, First Prize, Nantucket, MA
1969	Avalon Presidential Citation for Excellence in Poetry "While New Horizons Leap" and "Poem for a Sometime Day in Spring" Chinquapin Legacy Citation for Excellence of Expression for "Nocturne"
1970	World Poetry Society, distinguished Service Citation June 1, 1970

MEMBERSHIPS

1923-24	Member, Art Studio Club, Inc., New York, NY (80 West 40th Street)
1937	Member, American Abstract Artists
1941	Honorary Membership, Eugene Field Society, National Association of Authors and Journalists, St. Louis, MO
1958	Artists Association of Nantucket, Active Patron Member, The English-Speaking Union, New York, NY
1960	Member, The American Federation of the Arts, New York, NY
1965	Member, United Poetry Society of America
1970	Member, World Poetry Society
1970-71	Member, Artist Equity Association of New York, New York, NY
1970-72	Member, The Poetry Society of America
1971-72	Member, Avalon, Avalon World Arts Academy

Life Member, Munson-Williams-Proctor Institute

Life Member, Whitney Museum of American Art

Life Member, Museum of Modern Art

Member, American Abstract Artists Group

Member, Federation of Modern Painters and Sculptors

Member, Artist Equity Association

Member, Nantucket Art Association

MRG PUBLICATIONS

To purchase catalogues, please visit www.michaelrosenfeldart.com

MRG EXHIBITIONS

Facets of the Figure: A Spectrum of 20th Century American Art . . . . .June 5–August 22, 1997

Gallery II: Charles Seliger: Biomorphic Drawings, 1944-1947 . . . . .June 5–August 22, 1997

Bob Thompson: Heroes, Martyrs & Spectres . . . . .September 11–November 8, 1997

Gallery II: Alfonso Ossorio: The Shingle Figures, 1962-1963 . . . . .September 11–November 8, 1997

Burgoyne Diller: The Third Dimension, Sculpture & Drawings, 1930-1965 . . . . .November 13–January 17, 1998

Gallery II: The New Frontier: Early American Moderns . . . . .November 13–January 17, 1998

African-American Art: 20th Century Masterworks, V traveled to

The Newcomb Art Gallery, Tulane University, New Orleans, LA . . . . .January 22–March 21, 1998

Defining the Edge: Early American Abstraction, Selections from the

Collection of Dr. Peter B. Fischer traveled to The Laguna Art Museum, Laguna, CA . . . . .March 26–May 30, 1998

Essence of the Orb . . . . .June 4–August 20, 1998

Gallery II: Boris Margo: Divine Light, 1950-1952 . . . . .June 4–August 20, 1998

Alfonso Ossorio: Master Prints, 1932-1990 at Ossorio Foundation,

Southampton, NY . . . . .June 20–September 6, 1998

Betye Saar: Workers + Warriors: The Return of Aunt Jemima traveled

to Greenville County Museum of Art, Greenville, SC; Detroit Institute of

Arts, Detroit, MI . . . . .September 10–October 31, 1998

Gallery II: Spirit & Form: Charmion von Wiegand: Collages, 1946-1961 . . . . .September 10–October 31, 1998

Alfonso Ossorio, The Child Returns: 1950-Philippines, Expressionist

Paintings on Paper . . . . .November 5, 1998–January 9, 1999

Gallery II: Bob Thompson: Fantastic Visions, Paintings & Drawings . . . . .November 5, 1998–January 9, 1999

African-American Art: 20th Century Masterworks, VI traveled to

Flint Institute of Arts, Flint, MI . . . . .January 14–March 6, 1999

Charles Seliger: The Nascent Image, Recent Paintings . . . . .March 11–May 1, 1999

Gallery II: Morris Graves: Toward an Ultimate Reality . . . . .March 11–May 1, 1999

Linear Impulse May 6–August 13, 1999

Gallery II: Norman Lewis—Intuitive Markings, Works on Paper, 1945-1975 . . . . .May 6–August 13, 1999

Alfonso Ossorio: Costume Designs from the 1930s & 1940s for Ballet and

Greek Tragedies at Ossorio Foundation, Southampton, NY traveled to Mississippi

Museum of At, Jackson, MS . . . . .June 5–September 7, 1999

Beauford Delaney: Liquid Light—Paris Abstractions, 1954-1970 .September 10–October 30, 1999

Harold Cousins: The 1950s—Welded Sculpture . . . . .September 10–October 30, 1999

Burgoyne Diller: Collages . . . . .November 4, 1999–January 8, 2000

Gallery II: The Transcendental Painting Group . . . . .November 4, 1999–January 8, 2000

African-American Art: 20th Century Masterworks, VII traveled to Appleton

Museum of Art, Ocala, FL . . . . .January 13–March 4, 2000

True Grit traveled to Mills College Art Gallery, Oakland, CA; Boise Museum of Art,

Boise, ID; Marsh Art Gallery, University of Richmond, Richmond, VA; Farnsworth Art

Museum, Rockland, ME; El Paso Museum of Art, El Paso, TX; Newcomb Art Gallery,

Tulane University, New Orleans, LA; Center for the Visual Arts,

Metropolitan State College, Denver, CO . . . . .March 9–May 6, 2000

Gallery II: Betye Saar: In Service, A Version of Survival . . . . .March 9–May 6, 2000

Michael Rosenfeld Gallery: The First Decade . . . . .May 11–August 10, 2000

Alfonso Ossorio: The Creeks—Before, During and After at Ossorio Foundation,

Southampton, NY . . . . .June 1–September 4, 2000

Charmion von Wiegand: Spirituality in Abstraction, 1945-1969 .September 7–October 28, 2000

Gallery II: Blanche Lazzell: American Modernist . . . . .September 7–October 28, 2000

Nancy Grossman: Loud Whispers traveled to The Greenville County Museum of Art,

Greenville, SC; Savannah College of Art and Design, Savannah, GA . . . . .November 2, 2000–January 13, 2001

Gallery II: Sensual Lines: American Figurative Drawings . . . . .November 2, 2000–January 13, 2001

African-American Art: 20th Century Masterworks, VIII traveled to Texas Southern

University Museum, Houston, TX . . . . .January 18–March 10, 2001

Out of the Fifties—Into the Sixties: 6 Figurative Expressionists .March 15–May 5, 2001

Martha Madigan: Vernal Equinox, Recent Photograms . . . . .May 9–June 30, 2001

Gallery II: Flora: In Reverence of Nature . . . . .May 9–June 30, 2001

Synergy: Alfonso Ossorio and Jackson Pollock, 1950-1951 at Ossorio Foundation,

Southampton, NY traveled to Federal Reserve Fine Arts Program, Washington, DC June1–September 2, 2001

Alma Thomas: Phantasmagoria, Major Paintings traveled to

The Women's Museum, Dallas, TX . . . . .September 13–November 3, 2001

Gallery II: Abstraction on Paper, 1950–1965 . . . . .September 13–November 3, 2001

Burgoyne Diller: The 1930s, Cubism to Abstraction . . . . .November 8, 2001–January 12, 2002

94

CHECKLIST OF THE EXHIBITION

cover *Untitled (Cubist Still Life with Telephone II)* (MR30), c.1932
oil on canvas
24 x 20 inches, signed

p.20 *Untitled (Cubist Composition with Guitar)* (MR31), c.1932
oil on canvas
20 x 16 ¼ inches, signed

p.21 *Untitled (Cubist Composition with Telephone)* (MR32), c.1932
oil on canvas
24 x 20 inches, signed

p.19 *Untitled (Cubist Still-Life with Glass)* (MR33), c.1932
oil and sand on canvasboard
16 x 12 inches, signed

p.23 *Untitled (Cubist Teapot)*, c.1934
oil and sand on canvas
18 x 15 inches, signed

p.24 *Untitled (Conductor)* (MR50), c.1934
oil on canvas
30 x 22 inches, signed

p.25 *Untitled (Fourth of July)* (MR53), c.1934
oil on canvas
30 x 22 inches, signed

p.27 *Literary Blasphemes: Portrait of Ernest Boyd*, 1934
oil on canvas
28 x 24 inches
Private Collection, New York

p.70 *Untitled (Cubist Architectural Abstraction)* (MR40), c.1935
oil on canvas
18 x 15 ¼ inches, signed

p.30 *Untitled (Organic Cubist Abstraction)* (MR41), c.1935
oil on canvas
28 x 24 inches, signed

p.31 *Untitled (Organic Cubist Abstraction)* (MR42), c.1935
oil on canvas
36 x 30 inches, signed

p.33 *Untitled (Plastic Polygon Abstract Form)* (MR35), 1935
oil on canvas
28 x 24 inches, signed

p.39 *Untitled (Abstract Mask)* (MR36), 1935
oil on canvas
17 ⅛ x 15 ⅞ inches, signed

p.29 *Untitled* (MR37), 1935
oil and sand on canvas
28 x 24 inches, signed

p.34 *Untitled (Plastic Polygon Abstract Form)* (MR38), 1935
oil on canvas
28 x 24 inches, signed

p.37 *Untitled (Intersecting Trapezoids No.2)* (MR44), c.1936
oil on canvasboard
18 x 15 inches

p.6 *Untitled (Intersecting Trapezoids)* (MR45), c.1936
oil and sand on canvasboard
18 x 15 inches

p.38 *Untitled (Intersecting Trapezoids No.1)* (MR46), c.1936
oil and sand on canvasboard
18 x 15 inches

p.35 *Plastic Polygon Abstract Form "No. 6"* (MR43), 1936
oil on canvas
15 1/8 x 18 inches, signed

p.42 *Untitled (Red and Blue Abstraction)* (MR48), c.1937
oil on canvas
20 x 24 inches, signed

p.43 *Untitled (Polygon)* (MR49), c.1937
oil and sand on canvas
17 x 20 inches

p.45 *Untitled*, 1937
oil and sand on panel with artist frame
32 ¼ x 20 ¾ x 1 ½ inches
Private Collection, New York

p.41 *Polygon "No. 34"* (MR47), 1937
painted wood relief
22 ¼ x 28 ¼ x 1¾ inches, signed

p.4 *Untitled (Polygon Construction)* (MR54), 1939
painted wood relief
17 x 12 x 3 inches, signed

p.52 *Untitled* (MR21), c.1940
oil on canvasboard
20 x 16 inches, signed

p.47 *Untitled* (MR63), c.1940
oil on wood
11 x 16 ½ x 1 ¼ inches

p.49 *Untitled I* (MR20), 1940
oil on canvasboard
16 x 12 inches, signed

p.48 *Untitled* (MR26), 1940
oil on canvasboard
16 x 11 ⅞ inches, signed

p.53 *Untitled* (MR28), 1940
oil on canvasboard
16 x 12 inches, signed

p.51 *Non-Objective Organization - I* (MR55), 1940
oil on canvasboard
18 x 14 ¾ inches, signed

p.55 *Untitled* (MR23), 1941
oil on canvasboard
16 x 12 inches, signed

p.57 *Untitled (Geometric Abstraction)* (MR56), 1942
oil on Masonite
22 x 30 inches, signed

p.58 *Untitled (Atomic Flight)* (MR57), 1945
oil on canvasboard
22 x 30 inches, signed

p.59 *Atomic Flight* (MR58), 1946
oil on canvasboard
22 x 30 inches, signed

p.61 *Nantucket Wharf - No.2* (MR61), 1947
oil on canvasboard
30 x 22 inches, signed

p.63 *Nantucket Waterfront - No.3* (MR22), 1948
oil and sand on Masonite
50 x 32 inches, signed

95

CREDITS

Exhibition Coordinator	Michael Rosenfeld
Catalogue Design and Editor	halley k harrisburg
Catalogue Essay	© Debra Bricker Balken
Essay Editor	Jessica Scarlata
Chronology	Jason Andrew
Research Assistant	Sarah Kent
Catalogue Photography	Joshua Nefsky
Catalogue Art Direction and Production	CP Design
Catalogue Typeface	Kabel, Adobe Garamond
Catalogue Printing	Oceanic Graphic Printing, Inc.
Printed in China	Edition 1500
	ISBN #1-930416-42-3

© Michael Rosenfeld Gallery
24 West 57 Street, 7th Floor
New York, NY 10019
(212) 247-0082 / (212) 247-0402 fax
www.michaelrosenfeldart.com

Gallery Hours:
Tuesday through Saturday, 10:00-6:00

On the cover: *Untitled (Cubist Still Life with Telephone II)*, c.1932, oil on canvas, 24 x 20 inches, signed

All photographs of Charles G. Shaw used in this publication have been provided by the Archives of American Art, Smithsonian Institution, Washington, DC. They are courtesy of the Charles Green Shaw papers, 1874-1979.

Michael Rosenfeld Gallery extends sincere gratitude to Debra Bricker Balken, whose scholarship on Charles G. Shaw has secured his position in the history of twentieth century American art.

Research assistance and guidance were also generously provided by Ms. Wendy Hurlock Baker, Photo Order Co-ordinator of the Archives of American Art, Washington, DC; Ms. Stephanie Cassidy, Archivist at the Art Students League of New York; Ms. Pam Koob, Curator of the Collections at the Art Students League of New York; and Ms. Kristin Richards, Archive Assistant at the Whitney Museum of American Art Library.